D.L

Rob Thompson
Photography by Martin Thompson

The Manufacturing Guides

Sustainable Materials, Processes and Production

Thames & Hudson

Contents

Page 2, clockwise from top left: loom weaving wool by Mallalieu's of Delph; recycled blue and yellow plastic pipes by Smile Plastics; Nest of Tables by Ercol; mixed metal waste being recycled by Sims Recycling Solutions

Copyright © 2013 Rob Thompson and Martin Thompson

Designed by Christopher Perkins

First published in 2013 in paperback in the United States of America by Thames & Hudson Inc., 500 Fifth Avenue, New York, New York 10110

thamesandhudsonusa.com

Library of Congress Catalog Card Number 2012941710

ISBN 978-0-500-29071-2

Printed and bound in China by Toppan Leefung

Part One
Materials

How to use this book

This guidebook is intended to be a source of inspiration in the process of design for sustainability. The lifecycles of materials and products are covered, including raw material production, manufacturing and end-of-life. Many processes are explored in detail, including craft, mass production and emerging technology. The case studies demonstrate leading examples of sustainable practices and highlight the opportunities for designers.

How to use the processes sections
The book is divided into three parts (colour coded for ease of reference): materials are blue, processes are amber and lifecycle is green.

Each material and process is introduced with key reasons why it might be selected. For materials, the description focuses on the environmental impacts of production. Manufacturing processes are explored according to the requirements of designers: visual quality, typical applications, cost and speed, compatible materials and environmental impacts. For lifecycle, the impact of end-of-life on design, successful examples and the cost implications are considered.

The technical illustrations show the inner working of the technology. These principles define the technical constraints of the tools, equipment or typical set-up

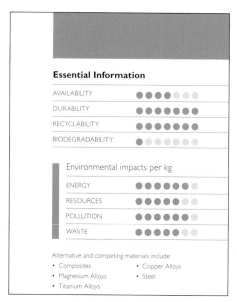

Essential information
A rough guide to the key features of each process to help inform designers and aid decision-making. The values are relative: 1 is low and 7 is high. Therefore, the most applicable and sustainable processes will have a greater number of dots in the top section and fewer dots in the section that relates to environmental impacts.

of a workshop. Each technique within a process – such as producing wool fabric, which includes shearing sheep, grading, scouring, dyeing, carding, combing and weaving, or water-based coating, which includes spray and dip techniques – is individually explored and technically explained.

How to use the essential information panels
The opening spread for each process includes a detailed essential information panel. This defines comparable values for the key factors that determine the impact of

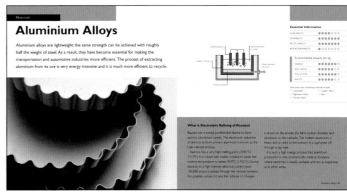

Processes and case studies Each process, including those used to produce raw materials, manufacture products or convert products back into raw materials at the end of their useful life, is described in detail. This example demonstrates the production of primary aluminium from mined bauxite ore, including the electrolytic reduction process.

each process on people and the environment: energy, resources, pollution and waste. Depending on whether the process is used to extract materials, make products or recycle them, end-of-life and additional comparable values are included. The scoring system is relative and based on one point being the lowest and seven points the highest. These values will be affected dramatically by the source, application and context of use. They are intended to be a rough guide to help inform designers and aid decision-making.

Related processes, such as the different stages and techniques used in screen printing (screen making and printing), are listed. In addition, potential alternative and competing processes – covered in this book or another book in the *Manufacturing Guides* series – are highlighted.

How to use the case studies

The real-life case studies feature material production, factories and workshops from around the world. They demonstrate some of the most innovative approaches to manufacturing sustainable products. Examples of leading products show how the finished article appears to the consumer.

Each process is covered by a step-by-step description and analysis of the key stages. The principal attributes of

each are described in detail and some of the extended qualities, such as scale and material scope, are outlined where necessary. Photographs of geometry, detail, colour and surface finish are used to show the many opportunities that each process has to offer.

Relevant links between the processes, such as materials and recycling, are highlighted in the text. It is essential that designers are aware of the wide range of opportunities at their disposal. This information provides a well-informed starting point for further focused investigation, which is fundamental to harnessing the full potential of materials and processes as a designer.

Introduction

This book is an optimistic and unbiased exploration of the sustainable practices of some of the most innovative factories. It provides an insight into materials production, manufacturing and recycling, and will help designers to take a progressively sustainable and low-carbon approach to product development, ensuring their projects have a positive impact on people and the environment.

Material lifecycle is considered, from forest and mine to the billets and granules delivered to the manufacturer. The production of metals, plastics, glass, textiles and wood is explored to provide an insight into the leading companies in this area. Many materials have a positive environmental impact, for example, natural fibres (page 94) can be grown organically and converted into high performance biocomposites (page 98), which are biodegradable at the end of their useful lives, returning nutrients back to the earth. However, the extraction of many types of material, especially metal ores, is inherently damaging to the environment. In such cases, recycled materials should be used wherever possible and the product should be designed to make the best use of those materials at the end of their lives.

Craft and industrial manufacturing processes are presented. These include traditional sustainable techniques, such as using local renewable materials

Bamboo packaging
Jiuxiang bamboo wine is packaged in the bamboo used to make it. The inside of the bamboo dissolves into the mix of sorghum, corn, wheat and spring water, creating a distinctive flavour. Bamboo is fast growing, renewable and sustainable (it does not require fungicide or pesticide).

(above), and mass production processes modified to accommodate more environmentally sustainable materials, such as injection molding (page 104). Many processes covered in other titles in the *Manufacturing Guides* series could be considered for sustainable product development: it depends on the inputs, process and outputs – and how they are fine-tuned to minimize or eliminate environmental impacts.

Recycled plastic granules
Many different types
of plastic are used in
everyday products.
Sophisticated processes
have had to be developed
to separate the subtly
different types. Now
it is also possible
to separate colour
groups to help maintain
high quality colour in
recycled products.

Paper Recycling, page 212 and Glass Recycling, page 216). Greater consideration for what happens to a product at the end of its life can ensure higher recovery rates: this improves efficiency and the likelihood of recovered materials being remanufactured into new products. Recycling processes are developing rapidly to cope with complex mixed waste streams: recycled plastics can be almost indistinguishable from virgin plastic (left).

Knowledge about design for sustainability

Design for sustainability is about considering the impact of a product or service on people and the environment throughout production, use and disposal.

In 1995 Designtex launched Climatex Lifecycle upholstery, the first biological nutrient textile, with McDonough Braungart Design Chemistry (MBDC) and the Rohner textile mill. The range of woven textiles demonstrates how, with consideration for the complete lifecycle, products manufactured using complex industrial processes can have a minimal, or even neutral, impact on people and the environment. Environmental regulation encourages sustainable development. There is also increasing pressure from stakeholders, such as consumers and Non-Government Organizations (NGOs), due to growing public awareness of environmental issues.

Products at the end of their useful lives are very valuable, so wherever possible they are reused, for instance as returnable packaging (page 194), or are recovered and refurbished, as with electronic products (page 186). This limits the amount of processing and so reduces the total environmental impact. If this is not an option, then material value is extracted by recycling (Mixed Recycling, page 198, Plastics Recycling, page 208,

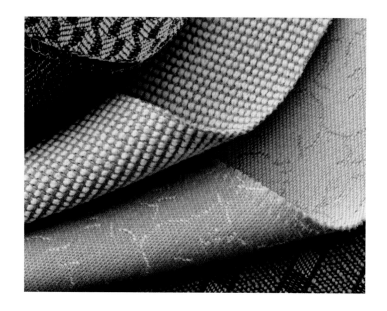

Environmental regulation Environmental laws and legislation are put in place to encourage the adoption of processes and technologies that reduce emissions, waste, consumption of resources and production of harmful materials. In the short term this can increase cost, especially if new equipment is needed, and noncompliance can result in hefty fines. Ultimately, though, reducing waste and improving efficiency saves money.

Legislation shifts responsibility, making individuals and organizations accountable for reducing the environmental impact of goods and services. For example, the End of Life Vehicles (ELV) Directive was introduced in Europe in September 2000. The aim is to manage the 8–9 million tons (17.5–20 million lbs) of vehicles decommissioned in Europe annually in a more environmentally friendly manner. To achieve this, producers are encouraged to make vehicles that are more readily dismantled and recycled, by standardizing parts, for instance, while reducing the use of harmful materials. In parallel, the recycling industry has set up suitable treatment sites with depollution, recovery and shredding facilities to meet the requirements of the directive (page 200). The Waste Electrical and Electronic Equipment (WEEE) Directive and Battery Directive have similar objectives (Mixed Recycling, page 198). The Environmental Protection Agency (EPA) enforces environmental initiatives in the US.

Environmental standards, labels and certifications Labels and certifications are used worldwide to identify environmentally sustainable products. This is especially useful for processes that have traditionally been criticized for damaging the environment, and materials and products originating from developing countries, where the health of people and the environment may not be so well protected.

Here is a brief overview of some of the most popular and most relevant to design. The Nordic Ecolabel (www.nordic-ecolabel.org), Blue Angel (www.blauer-engel.de) and EU Ecolabel (ec.europa.eu/environment/ecolabel) are used to mark products that meet extremely high environmental requirements based on lifecycle assessment (LCA). This includes an assessment of raw materials, production, use and disposal. Fairtrade promotes better prices, decent working conditions, local sustainability and fair terms of trade for farmers and workers in the developing world. The scheme includes agricultural products such as cotton (www.fairtrade.org.uk). Oeko-Tex Standard certifies that textiles do not contain any known harmful substances (www.oeko-tex.com). The Programme for the Endorsement of Forest Certification (PEFC) is the largest certification organization and promotes sustainable forest management (www.pefc.org). The Forest Stewardship Council (FSC) focuses on forest management and chain of custody certification. This allows consumers to identify, purchase and use timber and forest products from well-managed sources (www.fsc-uk.org).

Stakeholders Depletion of resources, global warming, pollution and man-made disasters raise public awareness about the impact we are having on the planet. In *Green to Gold*, published in 2006, Daniel C. Esty and Andrew S. Winston explain how companies can ride the 'green wave' and turn environmental challenges to their competitive advantage. There are many examples of businesses reducing their impact on the environment and increasing profits by meeting or exceeding the environmental demands of consumers.

NGOs play a crucial role in the process of regulation: they have instigated and continue to promote many environmental labels and certifications. There are many thousands in operation: the key players include Greenpeace (www.greenpeace.org), Friends of the Earth (www.foe.co.uk), National Wildlife Federation (www.nwf.org) and World Wildlife Fund (www.worldwildlife.org). They are founded on principals of protecting people, biodiversity and the planet's resources, and in most cases provide crucial critical input to business and government decision-making.

Life Cycle Assessment (LCA) Examining the total environmental impact of a product through every step of its life is known as lifecycle assessment (LCA). Values are determined for each stage: raw material production, transportation, manufacture, distribution, use and disposal. It is very useful when comparing products, but calculating precise values is extremely complex, especially if a product is made up of many materials from different sources and is distributed worldwide.

The total energy required to manufacture materials is referred to as embodied energy. It is used as a comparison by weight (MJ/kg) or volume (MJ/m³). The difficulty is that different material groups do not perform in the same way. In other words, light materials will likely have high MJ/kg and low MJ/m³. For example, plastic has higher MJ/kg and lower MJ/m³ compared to steel.

Wood products Engineered timber (page 62) products are made up of wood veneers, particles or core materials that are bonded together with strong adhesives at high pressure. They are strong, decorative and an efficient use of materials. The amount of energy required to make them will be higher than for sawn timber: birch plywood has three to five times more MJ/kg than kiln-dried birch. By contrast, air-dried wood has almost zero embodied energy and the tree stores carbon dioxide from the atmosphere as it grows.

Baskets Made from renewable natural materials – pine (top), birch bark (middle) and cane (bottom) – baskets have evolved to make the most of locally available materials. Basket weaving is utilized in the production of storage, packaging, furniture, bags and hats.

Generally, more expensive materials have higher embodied energy because they are more costly to produce. The precise value depends on the ingredients, how far the material was transported, the recycled content, energy use and so on. For example, stainless steel is relatively high cost, but can be recycled readily, so it is likely to be made up of several generations of recycled metal. By contrast, wood products may or may not be from certified sources, softwood, hardwood, coated or laminated, and the energy used in production may come from wood waste (above, left).

Materials

Material selection impacts heavily on the sustainability of products and services. Excluding the energy consumed by-products during their lifetime – for example, the greatest environmental impact of a vacuum cleaner or washing machine is the energy used in operation – materials may be the greatest environmental consideration because the extraction, processing and refinement can be energy intensive and polluting.

Natural materials, such as wood (page 56) and plant fibres (page 94), are manufactured into products with very little processing of the raw material. Wood can be air-dried, while basket weaving (page 132) makes use of local, renewable materials (above, right). Wool (page 84) is a beautiful and versatile material used to make upholstery (page 152) and clothing. It is naturally water-resistant, fire-resistant and a good insulator. Biocomposites (page 98) combine the properties of natural fibres with bioplastics (page 24) to produce high-performance parts that are lightweight, low cost and can be biodegradable (opposite, left).

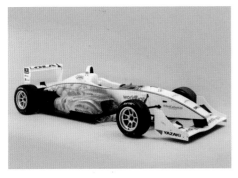

WorldFirst racing car Sponsored by the Warwick Innovative Manufacturing Research Centre (WIMRC) at Warwick Manufacturing Group, the WorldFirst racing car is designed and made from sustainable and renewable materials. The laminated composite bodywork is made of flax and recycled carbon fibre, and the steering wheel is a bioplastic reinforced with cellulose nanofibres from carrots and other root vegetables.

Flax composite Flax composite cones, manufactured by Lola using woven flax prepreg from Composites Evolution and Umeco, are rigorously tested at Warwick Manufacturing Group. These flax-reinforced plastics have similar energy absorption (by weight) to synthetic materials such as carbon and glass. Research continues and new material formulations are continually being developed.

The source of materials is critical. For example, leather (page 76) is a natural material and a by-product of meat production. Chrome tanning, used to cure the raw hide to make durable and long-lasting leather, has received criticism for causing pollution and using chrome (a common industrial material that is carcinogenic in some forms, but not in the one used for tanning). Some companies, such as Heinen Tannery, have, however, made huge progress in all production steps to reduce water and energy consumption and reuse or recycle chemicals and by-products. Industrial hemp is an important sustainable material that thrives in most climates with minimal pesticides and herbicides. The bast fibres used in textiles, papermaking and biocomposites, for example, are long, strong, durable, antimicrobial and biodegradable. However, cultivation is limited to only a handful of countries due to its close association with marijuana (a psychoactive drug).

Plastics are either derived from oil (see Plastics, page 20), bio-based (page 24) or semi-synthetic (see Cellulose Acetate, page 30 and Natural Rubber, page 36). Biodegradable plastics form another class of products that may or may not be bio-based. Depending on the type and source of material, bioplastics are not necessarily environmentally superior if factors such as genetic modification (GM), pesticides, fungicides and land use are taken into consideration.

Steel is the most common metal and is relatively energy efficient to produce: it requires approximately 50% less energy to make than plastic for the same weight of material. The production of metal alloys such as aluminium (page 44), magnesium and titanium is much more energy intensive. However, unlike plastics, metals can be recycled indefinitely. For example, recycling aluminium requires only 5% of the energy and produces only 5%

of the carbon dioxide equivalent emissions of primary aluminium production. The long-term effectiveness of metal recycling depends on how alloys are separated: there are many different grades of aluminium alloy, for example, ranging from soft and malleable to stiff and ductile, depending on the exact ingredients.

Glass is produced in a continuous process, 24 hours a day, 365 days a year. High temperatures are required, but the process is relatively efficient. There are several different types, but the most common is soda lime produced by the float glass process (page 52). Glass scrap, known as cullet, is mixed with the ingredients – silica sand, dolomite, lime and soda – to reduce the firing temperature required to make the raw material.

Processes

Manufacturers are continually improving efficiency: waste, energy and emissions are reduced to cut costs and satisfy new and evolving legislation. When considering the total environmental impact of a product, the priorities should align with good business practice.

Low-Volume and Batch Production Traditionally sustainable processes, such as weaving (page 92 and Basket Weaving, page 132), wood joinery (page 142), upholstery (page 152) and steam bending (page 136) are hands-on. This means less energy-consuming automated processes and less waste compared to mass production. The products are considered more valuable to consumers too, because the character of craftsmanship is visible in the finished article.

Screen printing (page 174) is used to apply graphics and colour to bags, T-shirts and packaging, for example. Water-based inks do not contain harmful chemicals, solvents or plastics. However, they are more difficult to work with than conventional inks and dry more rapidly. As a result, they have not been adopted widely, but are being utilized by a small number of forward-thinking printers. By contrast, water-based paints (page 158) have many advantages compared to solvent-based products: these include good visual quality, low cost, durability and no toxicity. They are being widely adopted in the furniture and automotive industry for all scales of application up to mass production.

Mass Production Injection molding (page 104) is the most widely used process for mass-producing plastic products. It is also used to mold bioplastics, which can have lower environmental impact than conventional plastics. They are therefore being used as a direct replacement.

Recycled plastics Molded by Smile Plastics, these colourful sheet materials are manufactured from recycled plastic (page 208). Ideally, materials are recycled into products of equal quality to maintain their value — for example, waste kayaks recycled into new kayaks (page 122).

Waterless printing Graphics and text can be reproduced more accurately with waterless printing because the ink is more viscous and held in place on the print cylinder by precisely etched pockets.

Material selection is key because, as with injection molding, many processes can be converted to accommodate more environmentally sustainable materials. Choosing an alternative material — unless it is a direct replacement — will mean taking a new approach to the design and engineering of the product. For example, recycled plastics can be molded with conventional processes but may require a change in part design and tooling (above, left).

The most exciting environmental manufacturing breakthroughs also improve the quality of a product. For example, waterless printing (page 182) is an emerging mass production printing process (above, right). Compared to offset lithography the unit costs are equivalent, reproduction quality is very high and can be more accurate, harmful emissions are reduced by 95% and water consumption is dramatically reduced.

Lifecycle

End-of-life is a critical consideration for developing more sustainable products. Natural materials, and even some synthetics (see Plastics, page 20), can be returned to the earth through composting. Technically, this means that more than 90% must be converted into carbon dioxide, water and biomass within 90 days. All materials will biodegrade, some much more slowly than others. Alternatively, waste material is burnt to generate energy. This can be carbon-neutral, such as burning wood waste to generate the energy required for the production of wood products, since burning wood puts back into the atmosphere only what was absorbed by the tree while it grew. Burning other waste materials has to be very carefully controlled because they are likely to contain harmful ingredients that can be released into the atmosphere, damaging people and the environment.

Recycling composite materials With current technology it is very difficult – impossible in most cases – to recycle 100% of materials if two or more are permanently joined together. The metal plating on this computer memory is the most valuable part: to reclaim it, the plastic is burnt away in the smelting process. In this way, the plastic is used as a fuel, aiding the metal recycling process.

Reduce Eliminating parts, materials, weight, useless waste and hazardous contents is both economically and environmentally beneficial. To be truly effective, all of the inputs should be considered and reduced to match the value that can be obtained from the product at the end of its life.

Reuse Avoiding sending parts to landfill is fundamental. If they can be reused without significant reprocessing this helps to reduce the total environmental impact (see Recover, Refurbish, Reuse, page 186). However, eventually they will be disposed of or recycled, and this needs to be considered.

Recycle In the past, materials of similar type – different grades of plastic, for example – were often mixed during recycling. Known as downcycling, this produced materials of inferior quality. Today, sophisticated processes are employed to separate all the materials carefully, so they can be effectively recycled to make high-quality raw materials that are in some cases indistinguishable from virgin material (see Mixed Recycling, page 198 and Plastics Recycling, page 208).

Materials that are permanently joined together are the most challenging to recycle (above and opposite, left). In contrast, using a single type of material, or fewer dissimilar materials, increases recovery rates. Plastics are available in many different forms: thus it is possible that a single type of plastic can be used to fulfil many different requirements. For automotive applications, this could mean making the stiff interior panels, carpet and other parts from a single type of plastic that is suitably versatile, such as polypropylene (opposite, right).

The following chapters provide many insights into how material suppliers, manufacturers and the recycling industry are developing. It is up to designers, equipped with the information and ideas presented on the following pages, to get stuck in and make sure their products have a positive and long-lasting impact on people and the environment.

Curv® polypropylene sheet
This lightweight material is made from 100%
polypropylene (PP). It combines drawn PP fibres
(anisotropic properties) into a self-reinforced sheet
material. This consolidation produces a material with
all the properties of sheet PP (such as excellent
impact resistance, even at very low temperatures)
with the added tensile strength of a drawn PP fibre.
This means that at the end of its useful life it is more
straightforward to process than composites such as
glass or carbon fibre-reinforced plastic.

FibreCycle Carbon fibre (CF) is expensive and
there are waste concerns as demand increases.
The FibreCycle research project, led by Umeco in
collaboration with Tilsatec, Sigmatex, NetComposites,
Exel Composites and the University of Leeds, has
developed a process for converting waste carbon
fibre into sliver (top), yarn, tape, woven fabrics (above),
non-crimp fabrics and prepreg materials. Press-molded
composite, comprising 50% recovered CF and 50%
thermoplastic, offers half the tensile strength and 90%
of the tensile modulus of an equivalent composite
based on virgin materials.

Materials

Plastics

Plastics are versatile: they offer high strength, low weight and a wide range of vivid colours are relatively affordable. Predominantly derived from crude oil, plastics can be recycled at the end of their life, or the energy they contain can be recovered by incineration.

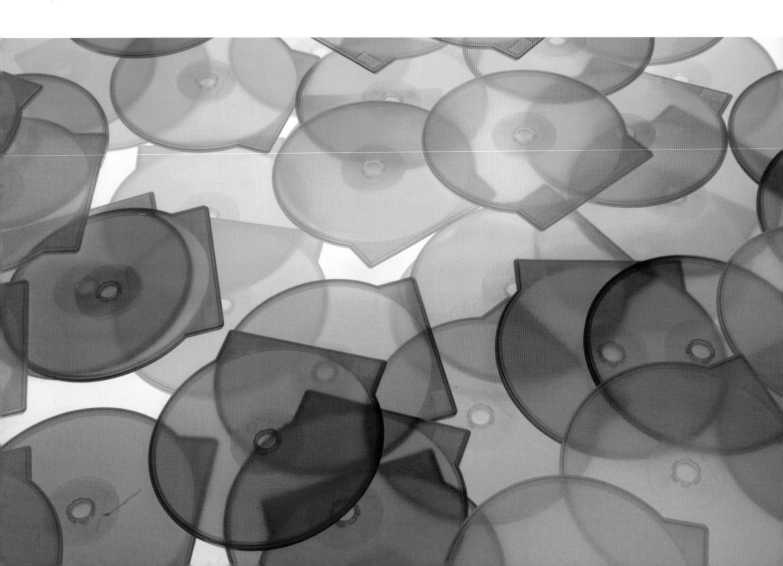

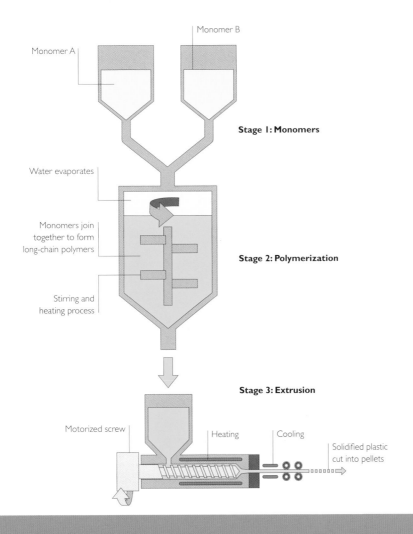

Monomer A

Monomer B

Stage 1: Monomers

Water evaporates

Monomers join
together to form
long-chain polymers

Stage 2: Polymerization

Stirring and
heating process

Stage 3: Extrusion

Motorized screw

Heating

Cooling

Solidified plastic
cut into pellets

Essential Information

AVAILABILITY	●●●●●○○
DURABILITY	●●●●●○○
RECYCLABILITY	●●●●●○○
BIODEGRADABILITY	●○○○○○○

Environmental impacts per kg

ENERGY	●●●●●○○
RESOURCES	●●●●○○○
POLLUTION	●●●●●○○
WASTE	●●●●○○○

Related materials include:
- Thermoplastic
- Thermosetting Plastic

Alternative and competing materials include:
- Glass
- Metal
- Paper and Board

What is Polymerization?

Synthetic plastics are polymers: long chains of repeating units (monomers). They are usually made from petrochemicals, which are derived from crude oil, but may also use bio-based building blocks derived from, for instance, corn, wheat or rice.

Raw crude oil is made up of many different types of hydrocarbons (compounds containing only hydrogen and carbon). Hydrocarbons of different molecular masses are separated by fractional distillation. One way in which monomers are obtained from the petroleum fractions, such as ethylene and propylene, is by cracking.

In this polymerization example (known as polycondensation), the monomers are fed into the reactor vessel in stage 1. In stage 2, they are heated and continuously stirred. They join together to form long polymer chains: over the course of 12 to 24 hours the water evaporates and the liquid mix becomes increasingly viscous. In stage 3, the polymer is extruded, cut into pellets and then dried for around 30 hours.

Notes on Environmental Impacts

The two main groups of plastics are thermoplastics and thermosetting plastics. The majority are derived from crude oil. Certain plastics may also be bio-based (below). These products are not always biodegradable and their environmental impact is not necessarily superior to that of conventional plastics if factors such as land and water use are taken into account. Biodegradable plastics form another class of products that may or may not be bio-based.

The environmental benefits of biodegradable plastics depend on the application. For example, they are an efficient way to contain and dispose of organic matter into municipal composting waste streams. This reduces the amount of solid waste going to landfill, which is a major environmental benefit. Special sorting systems can be used to ensure that biodegradable plastics do not contaminate recycling streams of other plastics.

With regards to eco-efficiency (overall environmental impact), energy recovery by incineration is often more effective than recycling plastics. Even so, thermoplastics can be recycled, but due to the processes and contamination their strength and quality will be slightly reduced each time, limiting the range of suitable applications. By contrast, thermosets form permanent cross-links between the polymer chains when molded. As a result, they cannot be directly recycled.

Plastics are often criticized for containing harmful ingredients. For example, phthalates and Bisphenol A are subject to restrictions in many countries. However, non-phthalate plasticizers are available for sensitive applications, such as toys and medical devices, made from PVC.

Biodegradable plastic Biodegradable petroleum-derived plastics are either compostable (partially bio-based) or oxy-degradable (contain photo-active or thermo-active ingredients). Oxy-degradable plastics fragment into tiny particles, but their biodegradability is not scientifically proven.

BASF Ecoflex® and Ecovio® are fully biodegradable plastics used in packaging applications. Ecoflex® is partially bio-based polyester: it has the properties of conventional polyethylene (PE), but is fully biodegradable under composting conditions. Ecovio® consists of polylactic acid (PLA) and Ecoflex®.

1

Case Study

Plastic Production from Crude Oil

Featured company BASF www.basf.com

Germany's Mittelplate oil field is at the southern edge of a Sea National Park in the tidal flats. Crude oil has been extracted in this sensitive production area without a single incident since 1987 (image **1**).

At the refinery the crude oil is cleaned and fractional distillation separates the different sizes of hydrocarbons. The resulting petrochemicals are broken down into olefins and aromatics by fluid catalytic cracking or steam cracking, which take place in large towers (image **2**). This is where ethylene and benzene, among other products, are extracted from the feedstock petroleum (naphtha). Both chemicals are used as raw materials in the production of styrene, which is employed in a range of plastics and foams. Plastics account for only around 5% of global oil consumption and the energy can be reclaimed by incineration or recycling (page 208) at the end of their life.

The raw ingredients – there are many thousands of types of plastic and the exact ingredients and processes for each are different – are mixed and polymerized. The plastic is compounded with additives, fillers and pigments for specific applications. In this case, the finished material is extruded (image **3**) and cut into pellets (image **4**).

2

3

4

Bio-based Plastics

Bio-based plastics are derived from renewable biomass sources, require less energy to manufacture than petroleum-derived plastics and are sometimes compostable. Either starch is used in its raw state, or it is further processed by bacterial fermentation to produce bio-based monomers, which are polymerized into bioplastics.

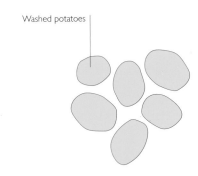

Washed potatoes

Stage 1: Harvest

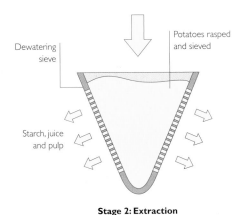

Dewatering sieve

Potatoes rasped and sieved

Starch, juice and pulp

Stage 2: Extraction

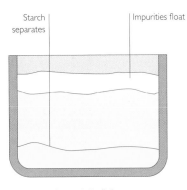

Starch separates

Impurities float

Stage 3: Refining

Essential Information

AVAILABILITY	●●●●○○○○○
DURABILITY	●●●●●●○○○
RECYCLABILITY	●●○○○○○○○
BIODEGRADABILITY	●●●●●●○○○

Environmental impacts per kg

ENERGY	●●●●○○○○○
RESOURCES	●●●●○○○○○
POLLUTION	●●●●○○○○○
WASTE	●●●○○○○○○

Related materials include:
- Polyhydroxyalkanoate (PHA) and Poly-beta-hydroxybutyrate (PHB)
- Polylactic Acid (PLA)   • Starch-based Biomaterials
- Thermoplastic Starch (TPS)

Alternative and competing materials include:
- Plastic

What is Starch Extraction?

Starch occurs naturally in plants such as potatoes, maize, wheat and rice, as well as others. Starch-based plastic is produced using the raw material, unlike bioplastics, which are produced by bacterial fermentation of starch (page 28) and polymerization (page 21). Raw starch is also used in papermaking to add strength (page 74), in textiles for added stiffness, and as sugar in processed food.

In stage 1, the plant is harvested and washed. In stage 2, the potatoes are wet-ground, rasped and sieved. This breaks down the tubular cells and releases the starch. The pulp passes through a powerful washing process and the resulting mix is sieved to separate the pulp, juice and starch.

In stage 3, the mix is washed repeatedly to separate the starch from the impurities, which float to the top as the starch settles. The starch is dried to form a white powder.

Notes on Environmental Impacts

Bio-based plastics are derived from biomass such as maize or potatoes. Their properties can be similar to petroleum-derived plastics, but they use 20% to 30% less energy to produce. They can be manufactured with conventional plastic-forming equipment, such as injection molding (page 104), blow molding, thermoforming and blown film extrusion.

Some are compostable, while others are biodegradable. Compostable means they fulfil US and EU standards (ASTM 6400 and EN 13432, respectively) for degrading in composting conditions (more than 90% must be converted into carbon dioxide, water and biomass within 90 days), whereas biodegradable simply means the material can be broken down into carbon dioxide, water and biomass by micro-organisms within a reasonable length of time.

The source of biomass is critical because the impact of growing the crops may outweigh the benefits – for instance, deforestation, genetic modification (GM), the use of petroleum-powered machinery for production and transportation, or the displacement of local food production and increased food prices.

Starch-based biodegradable packaging Starch-based plastics can contain 70% or more starch. The higher the starch content, the more rapidly the plastic will break down; high starch content plastics, such as this loose fill packaging (also known as packaging peanuts), will dissolve in water in 15 minutes or so.

Thermoplastic starch (TPS) cutlery Further processing of the raw starch by bacterial fermentation with yeast extract and glucose in water produces thermoplastic starch. This is a more durable and moldable material used to make cutlery, cast film, surgery gloves and woven textiles.

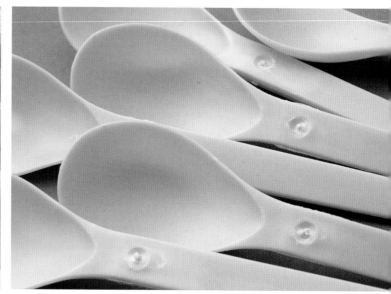

1

2

3

4

Case Study

Preparing PaperFoam Starch-based Plastic

Featured company PaperFoam www.paperfoam.com

White powder starch forms the basis for PaperFoam (image **1**). In the production of this bio-based material other ingredients, including long and short wood fibres, are added to provide strength (images **2** and **3**). Everything is combined in a food mixer (image **4**) with water, colouring and some proprietary ingredients. The typical ratios are 70% starch, 15% fibre reinforcement and 15% premix. The mixed material (image **5**) is ready to be formed by injection molding (page 104) or compression molding (page 110). The water causes it to foam when molded, resulting in stiff, lightweight parts.

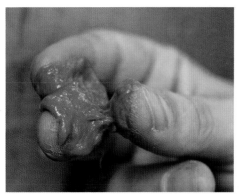

5

What is Bacterial Fermentation?

Starch contained in plants is converted into bio-based monomers by bacterial fermentation. The monomers are converted into bioplastics such as polyhydroxyalkanoate (PHA) and polylactic acid (PLA) by polymerization (page 21). This is a recent process and the technology is continually progressing through research and development.

Micro-organisms feed on the sugars in a bioreactor and multiply. When a sufficient quantity has been produced, the nutrient content is modified (such as limiting oxygen or nitrogen) and excess carbon is added, causing the bacteria to synthesize PHA, or lactic acid in the case of PLA. Depending on the micro-organisms and the cultivation process, many different types of bio-based monomer can be produced.

Following biosynthesis, the cell walls of the bacteria are broken down and the monomer is extracted and purified, ready for polymerization.

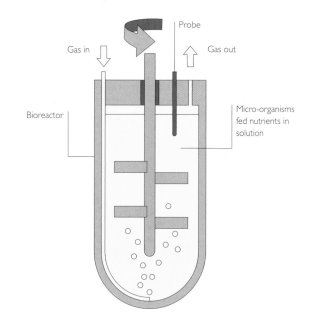

Probe

Gas in Gas out

Bioreactor

Micro-organisms fed nutrients in solution

Bioplastic production facility Production looks like a scientific laboratory and is in stark contrast to synthetic plastics. Bacterial fermentation is more commonly associated with making food – for instance, for yoghurt, sourdough bread and kimchi (Korean fermented cabbage).

A range of polymers is produced with varying properties. For example, PHA is commonly converted into poly-beta-hydroxybutyrate (PHB), which has similar properties to polypropylene (PP).

Case Study

Bioplastic Development

Featured company Bioresins www.bioresins.eu

These bioplastics have similar properties to conventional petroleum-based plastics. The granules (image **1**) are processed using conventional plastic-forming equipment including injection molding (page 104), blow molding, extrusion and blown film. They are also laminated and molded as biocomposites (page 98).

Properties range from stiff and rigid to flexible. PHA and PLA are recent developments and so are relatively expensive compared to commodity polymers such as polypropylene (PP) and polyethylene (PE): PLA is twice the price and PHA is about four times more expensive, taking into account the density changes.

It is used to make bottles (image **2**), packaging film (image **3**), toys, cutlery, stationery, composites and consumer electronic parts; many more applications are being explored as the demand for natural, renewable material increases. PHA has similar properties to PP or polystyrene (PS) depending on the exact ingredients. PLA, however, has similar properties to PS or polyethylene terephthalate (PET), which is commonly used in drink bottles. PHA, poly-beta-hydroxybutyrate (PHB) and PLA are fully biodegradable in microbial active environments.

Cellulose Acetate

This semi-synthetic plastic is derived from cotton fibres and wood pulp. It is shaped by calendaring, block pressing, injection molding, extrusion, machining – or by a combination of these processes. Craftsmanship and industrial techniques produce intricate patterns and colour effects that would otherwise be inconceivable in plastic.

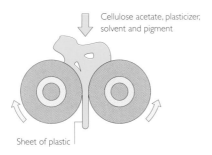

Cellulose acetate, plasticizer, solvent and pigment

Sheet of plastic

Stage 1: Mixing and calendaring

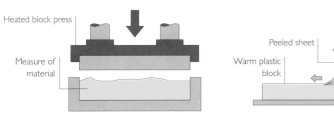

Heated block press

Measure of material

Stage 2: Block pressing

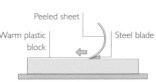

Peeled sheet

Warm plastic block

Steel blade

Stage 3: Slicing

Essential Information

AVAILABILITY	●●●●○○○
DURABILITY	●●●●◐○○
RECYCLABILITY	●●●●●●●
BIODEGRADABILITY	●●●●●●●

Environmental impacts per kg	
ENERGY	●●●●●◐○○
RESOURCES	●●●○○○○
POLLUTION	●●●○○○○
WASTE	●●●○○○○

Alternative and competing materials include:
- Plastic
- Wood

What is Block Processing?

In preparation, cellulose acetate powder is combined with plasticizer and solvent to make it soft and pliable. This produces a homogeneous paste that is filtered to remove impurities and to ensure that the best colour can be achieved.

The paste is mixed with pigment and calendared between two rotating cylinders. This makes a sheet material suitable for block pressing or cutting and laminating to create 3D, decorative coloured effects (page 33).

In a second step, a predetermined quantity of material is loaded into the block press. It is heated and, with pressure, the plastic consolidates and hardens to form a solid block. While it is still warm, which makes processing easier, sheets are sliced from it. These are either used as they are or laminated and re-pressed.

Notes on Environmental Impacts

Cellulose has been used in the production of plastics for more than a century. It is derived from cotton and wood, which should be from renewable and certified sources (see Wood, page 56). Cellulose-based plastics are typically made from chemically modified cellulose, using acetic acid: up to 70% of the finished material is composed of plant-based components. The most common type is cellulose acetate (CA): it is used in high quality eyewear frames (opposite) because it feels good next to the skin. Other applications include packaging films, filters, adhesives, coatings, papermaking (page 74) and textiles (see Weaving, page 92). Cellulose acetate is recyclable and fully biodegradable under controlled composting conditions.

The production of cellulose-based plastics is continually developing to reduce the environmental impacts. A notable example is M49® cellulose acetate, which is manufactured by Mazzucchelli and uses a plasticizer derived from biomass (as opposed to petroleum) and does not include phthalates (see case study, below).

Case Study

Forming Tortoiseshell-effect with Cellulose Acetate

Featured company Mazzucchelli
www.mazzucchelli1849.it

The cellulose acetate, which is identical in appearance but has a slightly different chemical composition to the extrusion powder (page 117), is mixed with solvent, plasticizer and pigment. The soft paste is mixed between two heavy rolls (images 1 and 2). The three shades of brown that will be used to make tortoiseshell-effect are carefully controlled. It is a highly skilled process because the quality of the finished sheet will be determined by the consistency of colour and concentration of mix.

The colours are cut into cubes (image 3), which are then spread out in the block press. After around a day the 250 kg (551 lbs) block is removed from the press (image 4).

Sheets are sliced from the block (image 5). The material is flexible at this stage because it is warm and still contains solvent. The solvent is removed by drying it in an oven at 55°C (131°F) for 15 days or so. Afterwards it is re-pressed to make it flat. Eyewear frames are cut from the sheet using CNC machining (image 6).

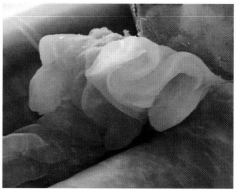

4

3

5

6

What is Decorative Block Pressing?

Cellulose acetate formed by calendaring or the block process (page 31) is cut into pieces or sheets and placed back inside the press. The process is the same except that the material will look very different when it is finished. In principal, each piece of material will be unique because the molds are prepared by hand.

Laminating is used to combine sheets that have printed details on the surface, thus encapsulating the layer of print inside the block. Laying coloured and patterned sheets at an angle will produce dramatic and 3D effects in the block. However, pressing pieces of plastic that are variations on a colour will produce a mottled appearance, similar to wood grain or pearl.

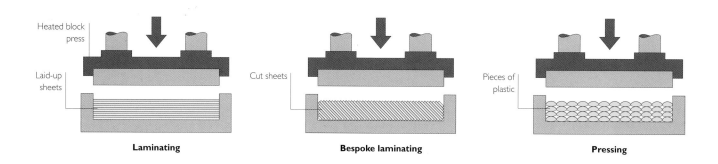

Heated block press

Laid-up sheets

Laminating

Cut sheets

Bespoke laminating

Pieces of plastic

Pressing

Case Study

Handcrafted Cellulose Acetate Sheets

Featured company Mazzucchelli
www.mazzucchelli1849.it

Cellulose was originally developed as an alternative to tortoiseshell and horn. The processes have evolved through the combination of highly skilled craft and industrial techniques. As a result, it is now considered a valuable material in its own right. This has been largely due to Mazzucchelli, who are a leading supplier to the eyewear industry and have been in operation in Italy since 1849.

The tortoiseshell material manufactured by block pressing (page 31) is cut into strips, laminated with white sheets, re-cut and re-pressed to form a grid-like structure. The transparency of the material means that the appearance changes according to the viewing angle and light transmission (images **1** and **2**). Materials of this nature take around 25 days to manufacture.

Designers can select patterns and effects from Mazzucchelli's vast back catalogue. Once they have selected an approach, many variations can be created, such as this combination of red and transparent

(image **3**). Creating geometric patterns in the mold requires a great deal of skill because misalignment will show up in the final material.

Non-geometric patterns are produced by laying up the sheets more randomly (image **4**). In this way almost any coloured effect can be achieved. Alternatively, sheets are printed and laminated onto one another. This technique is used to reproduce very precise graphics (image **5**).

1

2

3

4

5

Natural Rubber

Latex and rubber are elastomeric: they return to their original shape after stretching. Latex is tapped from rubber trees and is either used for coating or dip molding products such as gloves, balloons and condoms, or is further processed into rubber, a high-strength elastomer used in tyres and footwear.

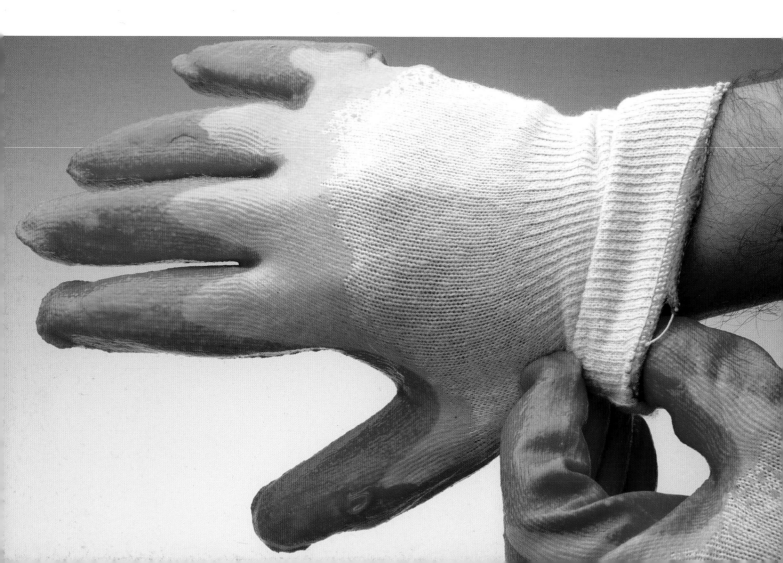

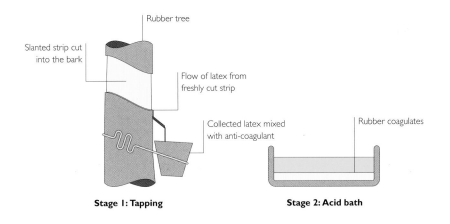

Stage 1: Tapping

Rubber tree

Slanted strip cut into the bark

Flow of latex from freshly cut strip

Collected latex mixed with anti-coagulant

Stage 2: Acid bath

Rubber coagulates

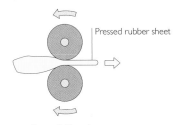

Pressed rubber sheet

Stage 3: Pressing

Essential Information

AVAILABILITY	●●●●●○○
DURABILITY	●●●●●○○
RECYCLABILITY	●●○○○○○
BIODEGRADABILITY	●○○○○○○

Environmental impacts per kg

ENERGY	●●●●○○○
RESOURCES	●●○○○○○
POLLUTION	●●●○○○○
WASTE	●●●○○○○

Related materials include:
- Latex
- Natural Rubber (NR)

Alternative and competing materials include:
- Bioplastic
- Cellulose Acetate (CA)
- Plastic (synthetic rubber, silicone, thermoplastic elastomer and polyurethane resin)

What is Latex and Rubber Production?

Tapping rubber trees is a highly skilled process. In stage 1, the worker cuts a 30° angle slot about 2 mm (0.08 in.) into the bark around one side of the tree. This wounds the bark and causes it to excrete latex. If the cut is too deep it could damage the tree and if it is too shallow the flow of latex will be reduced. The latex is collected in a cup and mixed with an ammonia solution to stop coagulation. At this point, the latex is either collected and transported for processing into concentrated latex, or further processed to make rubber.

In order to produce rubber sheets in stage 2, the latex is sieved to remove contamination and mixed with acetic or formic acid. Over several hours the rubber coagulates to form a soft rubber paste. In stage 3, after drying for 18 hours or so, the soft rubber is passed through a series of rollers to remove excess moisture and prepare it for vulcanization.

Notes on Environmental Impacts

Natural rubber (NR) can be fairtrade and certified by the Forest Stewardship Council (FSC): for instance, GreeTips's elastic bands and wellington boots from Sri Lanka (see page 112).

In general, NR is used for a wide range of products such as footwear, tyres, tubes, industrial belts, sports equipment and insulated cable. Many of these products, especially tyres, make a significant contribution to landfill and they will take many hundreds of years to break down.

Rubber is a thermoset material – strong cross-links are formed between the polymer chains during vulcanization – and it is therefore not possible to recycle directly. Unlike thermoplastics (page 22), which can be melted and reprocessed using relatively little additional energy, latex and rubber are shredded. The recycled material, known as 'crumb', is used as a filler material for shock-absorbing floors (such as playgrounds), insulation, asphalt and aggregate.

Developments include blending rubber with a thermoplastic to make an elastomer with a mixture of properties from both materials, which can be reprocessed by melting and molding. The possibility of devulcanizing cured rubber after shredding has also been explored, but not yet optimized and commercialized.

Some people are allergic to the proteins in latex; in the most extreme cases the reaction can be life threatening.

Case Study

Tapping Latex and Vulcanizing Rubber Sheets in Malaysia

A new cut is made at the bottom of the cut area of the bark (image **1**). This is repeated three to four hours later. The fresh cut will produce latex for several more hours (image **2**). Properly managed in this way, rubber trees will produce latex for around 25 years.

Production is carried out in the forest, amid the plantation, either by small producers or in large plantation factories. The latex is mixed with acid to produce soft, gelatinous rubber. After drying for several hours, excess moisture is pressed out by treading on the soft rubber (image **3**). The roughly formed sheet is then passed through a series of textured rollers (images **4** and **5**). At this point the rubber will deform easily: it can be formed by extrusion or compression molding (page 110), for example, or it can be vulcanized in sheet form.

Vulcanizing is carried out in a smokehouse (image **6**). After being exposed to sulphur for several days, cross-links are formed in the rubber, causing it to become a more stable, durable, resilient and long-lasting elastomer. This is known as 'Ribbed Smoked Rubber' (image **7**). Other common types include graded and standardized 'Vulcanized Rubber', 'Pale Crepe' for making shoe soles, 'Hevea Crumb' pressed rubber particles and 'Skim Rubber', which is lower quality.

1

2

4

5

3

6

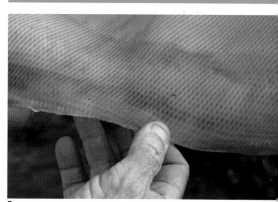

7

Steel

Steels are the most common metals and can be found in many industrial and domestic applications. They are relatively energy efficient to make and are readily recycled. Metals retain their full strength when they are recycled. Therefore, they can be reshaped many times without loss of quality or performance.

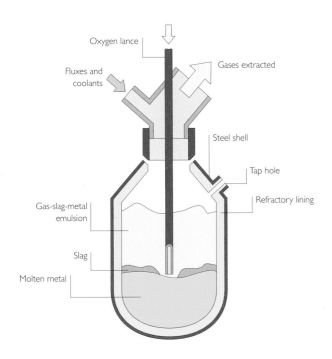

Oxygen lance

Fluxes and coolants

Gases extracted

Steel shell

Tap hole

Refractory lining

Gas-slag-metal emulsion

Slag

Molten metal

Essential Information

AVAILABILITY	●●●●○○○○
DURABILITY	●●●●●●●○
RECYCLABILITY	●●●●●●●○
BIODEGRADABILITY	●●○○○○○○

Environmental impacts per kg

ENERGY	●●●●●○○○
RESOURCES	●●●●●○○○
POLLUTION	●●●●●●○○
WASTE	●●●●●●●○

Related materials include:

- Carbon Steel
- Low Alloy Steel
- Tool Steel
- Iron
- Stainless Steel

Alternative and competing materials include:

- Aluminium Alloys
- Copper Alloys

What is Basic Oxygen Steelmaking?

Basic oxygen steelmaking (BOS), also known as the basic oxygen process (BOP), is the main bulk production process for refining pig iron into steel.

Pig iron is produced by heating crushed iron ore, coke and limestone in a blast furnace to 1600°C (2912°F). It is mixed with around 20% steel scrap in the BOS vessel and a supersonic jet of almost pure oxygen is blown through the oxygen lance onto the surface of the mixture. This causes carbon, silicon and other impurities in the pig iron to oxidize and generate 1700°C (3092°F) of heat, which melts the scrap.

Flux is fed in to form slag, which absorbs impurities from the molten metal. It is separated and used in, for example, asphalt aggregate and cement manufacturing. Around 350 tons (771,000 lbs) of steel is produced in each 30-minute cycle. The vessel is tipped and the steel drained from the tap hole.

Notes on Environmental Impacts

There are many types of steel including carbon (mild), stainless, low alloy and tool. This makes it a versatile and widely used material in construction, automotive, furniture and electronics products.

The production of steel is relatively energy efficient and there has been continuous improvement with efficiency savings made in production: energy consumption and waste have been reduced, by-products are reused and metal scrap is recycled. Even so, the processes are energy and carbon intensive, create pollution and hazardous by-products, and produce a lot of waste. Steel production alone accounts for around 3% of global carbon dioxide emissions, and about 284,000 litres (75,000 gallons) of water are required to make 1 ton (2,204 lbs) of steel.

Carbon steels are prone to oxidization and corrosion, so are typically protected with a coating such as galvanization, powder coating or painting (page 158). Low alloy and stainless steels contain alloying elements such as nickel and chromium.

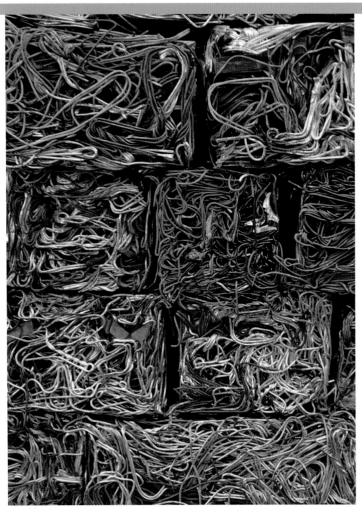

Scrap steel Recycling is inherent in steel production: all modern steel mills use recycled content to reduce energy consumption, emissions and resources. Recycling 1000 kg (2205 lbs) of steel saves roughly 1500 kg (3307 lbs) of ore, 500 kg (1102 lbs) of coal and 75% of the energy required to make primary steel. This reduces costs and thus scrap metals have significant economic value. Steel is easily separated from mixed waste streams (see Mixed Recycling, page 198) because it is magnetic.

1

2

3

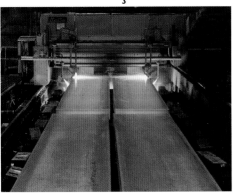

4

5

Case Study

Producing Steel from Iron Ore

Featured company United States Steel Corporation
www.ussteel.com

The iron ore, which in this case is taconite (an iron-bearing sedimentary rock), is mined (image **1**), crushed, pulverized and then processed into pellets for the blast furnace. Coal used to make coke is shipped to the steelworks (image **2**).

Pig iron is produced in a blast furnace and moved to the basic oxygen process shop, where slag is removed from the surface (image **3**) before the molten metal is transferred, using a ladle, to the basic oxygen process furnace. There, iron is refined into steel and alloys are introduced to produce the required mechanical properties.

The molten steel is continuously cast into billets, blooms or slabs and cut to length using gas torches (image **4**). They are either finished by hot rolling them into the finished profile or further processed by cold rolling (image **5**). Cold rolling is used to produce thinner strips, down to 0.15 mm (0.006 in.), which can then be coated with zinc (corrosion protection), tin (for packaging) or paint (protection and decoration).

Aluminium Alloys

Aluminium alloys are lightweight: the same strength can be achieved with roughly half the weight of steel. As a result, they have become essential for making the transportation and automotive industries more efficient. The process of extracting aluminium from its ore is very energy intensive and it is much more efficient to recycle.

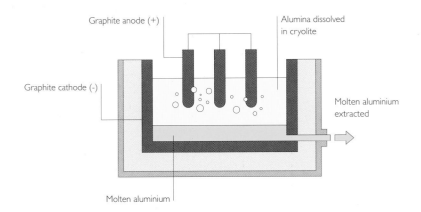

Graphite anode (+)

Alumina dissolved in cryolite

Graphite cathode (-)

Molten aluminium extracted

Molten aluminium

What is Electrolytic Refining of Alumina?

Bauxite ore is mined, purified and heated to form alumina (aluminium oxide). The electrolytic reduction of alumina to form primary aluminium is known as the Hall–Héroult process.

Alumina has a very high melting point (2045°C/3713°F). It is mixed with molten cryolite to lower the melting temperature to below 950°C (1742°F). During electrolysis a high intensity electrical current (over 100,000 amps) is passed through the mixture between the graphite anode (+) and the cathode (-). Oxygen is drawn to the anodes (to form carbon dioxide) and aluminium to the cathode. The molten aluminium is heavy and so sinks to the bottom. It is syphoned off through a tap hole.

It is such a high energy process that aluminium production is only economically viable in locations where electricity is readily available and not as expensive as in other areas.

Notes on Environmental Impacts

Bauxite ore is an abundant material and it takes only 4 kg (8.8 lbs) of alumina to make 1 kg (2.2 lbs) of aluminium, but the production of primary aluminium is such a high energy process that it is typically more expensive than steel. However, recycling aluminium is an energy efficient process and it is estimated that the aluminium used in one drink can will be used in another can only 60 days after it has been put in a recycling bin.

Pure aluminium is quite soft and ductile. It is therefore alloyed with small amounts of copper, manganese, silicon, magnesium and zinc to improve hardness and durability.

It has good strength to weight: the same strength can be achieved with roughly half the weight of aluminium compared to steel. In the presence of oxygen, the surface reacts to form a protective layer that makes it almost maintenance free. The protective layer is enhanced and can be coloured using the anodizing process.

Recycled aluminium The Emeco Hudson Heritage Stacking Chair by Philippe Starck uses 80% recycled aluminium. Recycling requires only 5% of the energy, is carried out at lower temperatures – the melting point of aluminium is 660°C (1220°F) – and produces only 5% of the carbon dioxide of primary aluminium production.

1

2

Extracting Primary Aluminium from Bauxite

Featured company Hydro www.hydro.com

Bauxite ore is mined and unloaded (image **1**). It is dissolved in caustic soda to produce aluminium hydroxide and to separate the unwanted elements. The aluminium hydroxide is heated (calcination) to produce a white alumina powder.

Primary aluminium is produced in smelting plants (image **2**). The electrolytic cells (also known as pots) are filled with the alumina and cryolite and heated to 950°C (1742°F) (image **3**).

The primary aluminium is siphoned off. It is combined with other elements (manganese, zinc, copper and so on) to create alloys with correct properties for the end application. It is cast into ingots, such as extrusion billets (image **4**), rolled products or strips.

3

4

Copper Alloys

Copper develops a protective and decorative patina on its surface when exposed to the atmosphere. It is reddish pink when first produced, becoming dark brown and eventually green. With prolonged exposure, the film becomes very durable and protective. This means the copper is maintenance-free and long-lasting.

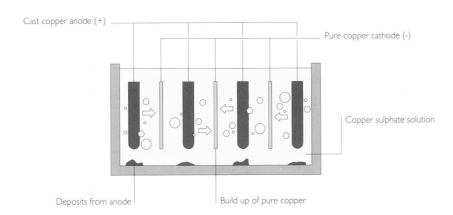

Cast copper anode (+)

Pure copper cathode (-)

Copper sulphate solution

Deposits from anode

Build up of pure copper

AVAILABILITY	●●○○○○○○
DURABILITY	●●●●●●○
RECYCLABILITY	●●●●●○●
BIODEGRADABILITY	●○○○○○○

Environmental impacts per kg

ENERGY	●●●●●○○
RESOURCES	●●●●●●○
POLLUTION	●●●●●○○
WASTE	●●●●●●○

Related materials include:
- Brass
- Copper
- Bronze

Alternative and competing materials include:
- Aluminium Alloys
- Steel

What is Electroextraction of Copper?

Electroextraction, or electrowinning, is an electrolytic process used to extract non-ferrous metals – such as copper, gold, silver, magnesium, lead and zinc – from ores in solution. In the case of aluminium production it is known as the Hall–Héroult process (page 45) and in the case of titanium, it forms part of the Kroll process.

Copper is obtained from its ore and cast into ingots. At this stage it has many impurities, including silver, gold and platinum. The ingots are loaded into the electroextraction tank and positively charged (anodes).

Pure copper sheet is interleaved between the anodes and grounded (cathodes). During electrolysis copper dissolves from the anodes into the copper sulphate solution and builds up as a pure copper coating on the cathode. The impurities collect as deposits and are removed and processed.

Notes on Environmental Impacts

Mining has a significant impact on the environment and companies have to follow strict guidelines that help to minimize air, water and soil pollution, and loss of biodiversity. Substantial waste is inevitable because ore is only a small fraction of the total volume of material mined. For example, it takes approximately 1 ton (2,204 lbs) of ore to yield 1 kg (2.2 lbs) or so of copper.

Using scrap metal in manufacturing uses significantly less energy and metals can be reprocessed without loss of quality or properties. As a result, most products and parts made from copper alloys contain recycled content.

Brass is an alloy of copper and 5% to 45% zinc. A greenish-brown patina develops on its surface and becomes dark brown over time. There are many different types of brass, which are categorized by the quantity of zinc. Higher levels of zinc produce harder and more brittle brasses. Bronze is an alloy of copper and up to 40% tin. The patina develops much more slowly and is a brownish colour.

Scrap copper for recycling Roughly one-third of the Aurubis Group's copper production originates in copper scrap. It is a widely used metal and the most common after iron (see Steel, page 40) and aluminium (page 44). Recycling is a fundamental part of primary copper production and helps to reduce the energy required and waste produced. This is essential because copper concentration is very low in mined ore.

Case Study

Primary Copper Production

Featured company Aurubis Group www.aurubis.com

The copper ore raw material is extracted in open-cast and deep mining (image **1**). It is derived from sulphide ores or oxide ores and the typical concentration is below 1%. Through a series of grinding, floating, smelting and roasting processes the impurities are gradually removed and the concentration increased to 99%. This material is cast into anodes in a carousel of molds (image **2**).

The anodes are placed into the electroextraction tanks, which are known as tankhouse cells. The copper cathodes are coated with pure copper and hoisted from the cell (image **3**). The finished billets are ready to be manufactured into new products (image **4**).

1

2

3

4

Glass

There are several types of glass including soda lime, lead alkali, borosilicate, aluminosilicate and glass ceramic. Each group has its own distinctive properties, which vary according to the manufacturer. In most cases the ingredients are mixed, melted and then formed into finished products in a continuous process.

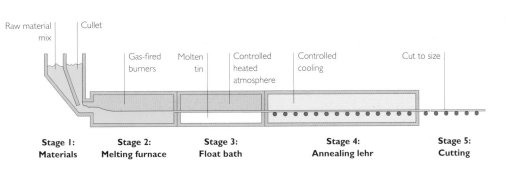

Raw material mix · Cullet

Stage 1: Gas-fired burners · Molten tin · Controlled heated atmosphere · Controlled cooling · Cut to size

Stage 1: **Materials**
Stage 2: **Melting furnace**
Stage 3: **Float bath**
Stage 4: **Annealing lehr**
Stage 5: **Cutting**

What is the Float Glass Process?

Float glass is soda-lime glass with slightly modified ingredients to make it suitable for mass production. The process was developed by Alastair Pilkington and production began in 1959. It has since become the standard method for mass producing flat glass and is now widely used in the construction and automotive industries.

It is produced in a five-stage process. In stage 1, silica sand, lime, dolomite and soda are mixed with cullet (recycled glass). In stage 2, the mix is heated by burning a combination of natural gas and pre-heated air at 1600°C (2912°F). In stage 3, the hot molten glass leaves the furnace at approximately 1000°C (1832°F) and is floated on a bath of molten tin in a controlled atmosphere of hydrogen and nitrogen that prevents the tin from oxidizing. In stage 4, the glass is annealed and cooled. In stage 5, the continuous sheet is cut to size.

Notes on Environmental Impacts

Production is continuous: the temperature is maintained every day, all year round. Manufacturing directly from mixed raw materials eliminates inefficiencies associated with widely distributed production such as plastics (page 20) and metals (see Steel, page 40, Aluminium Alloys, page 44 and Copper Alloys, page 48). This means that glass can have a lower environmental impact than plastic.

Modifications, such as coatings, are applied during production for specific functional improvements. Examples include self-cleaning Pilkington Activ™ produced by a very thin coating of titanium oxide; low emissivity Pilkington K Glass™, which reflects heat back into buildings and so reduces heat loss; and Pilkington Optifloat™ (see below), which has a higher level of clarity.

Mass production glassblowing (above) Blown and pressed products are manufactured with glass taken directly from the furnace (these processes are included in *Product and Furniture Design*). Like the float glass process, the furnace is in continuous use until it needs to be serviced or rebuilt.

Mall at Millenia (left) Designed by JPRA Architects, the Mall at Millenia in Florida utilizes Pilkington Optifloat™. It is ideal for facades and furniture due to a higher level of clarity than 'clear' glass.

Case Study

Manufacturing Soda-lime Glass

Featured company Pilkington Group Limited
www.pilkington.com

Soda lime is the most popular glass material. It is used in a wide variety of applications: flat glass, including windows and facades; blown glass, including packaging and sculpture; and pressed glass, including tableware. Soda lime, borosilicate and aluminosilicate glass can be produced using the float glass process.

The ingredients are mixed together and fed into the furnace (image **1**). It is a gradual process and the raw materials can take two to three days to pass through the furnace (image **2**). Once molten, the glass is floated on a bath of molten tin (image **3**), gripped by rollers. The speed of the rollers determines the thickness of the glass, producing up to 5,500 tons (12 million lbs) per week. The glass is manufactured as a continuous sheet (image **4**), which is cut to size according to customer requirements.

1

2

3

4

Wood

Wood has a minimal impact on the environment. In fact, the energy used in its production may be less than that stored in the wood by photosynthesis during its lifetime. Spruce, pine and birch are some of the most commonly used and are available from renewable sources.

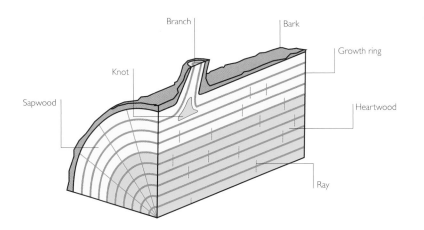

Branch | Bark | Growth ring | Knot | Sapwood | Heartwood | Ray

Essential Information

AVAILABILITY	●●●●●●○○
DURABILITY	●●●●●●○○
RECYCLABILITY	●●●●●●○○
BIODEGRADABILITY	●●●●●●●●

Environmental impacts per kg

ENERGY	●●●●●●●●
RESOURCES	●●●●●●●●
POLLUTION	●●●●●●●●
WASTE	●●●●●●●●

Alternative and competing materials include:
- Concrete
- Metal
- Engineered Timber
- Plastic

What is the Anatomy of Wood?

The strength and appearance of lumber (sawn timber) is determined by many important factors. These include the type of tree, potential defects, the method of drying and how it was cut at the sawmill (page 61).

Wood grain is produced by growth rings and rays. These are made up of cell structures that transport water and nutrients around the tree. Annual growth rings develop as a consequence of seasonal change and can be used to tell the age of a tree. Early in the growing season tree growth is rapid and the wood is typically lighter in colour because the cells are larger. Darker rings indicate slower growth from later in the growing season. Rings are intersected with rays, which are structures radiating from the centre of the tree to transport food and waste laterally. The combination of rings and rays produces patterns and flecks of colour on the surface of lumber.

As a tree matures the centre darkens: this is known as heartwood; the lighter wood near the bark is sapwood. The depth of sapwood and colour contrast depend on the species of tree.

Notes on Environmental Impacts

Wood is an environmentally beneficial material. It is non-polluting, biodegradable and can be recycled or used as biofuel at the end of its life. In most cases, the energy used to harvest, convert and transport wood is less than the energy it has stored by photosynthesis. Each 1 m³ (35.3 ft³) of tree growth absorbs around 0.9 tons (1,984 lbs) of carbon dioxide, so replacing materials such as concrete or steel with wood can significantly reduce carbon dioxide emissions. Certification schemes, such as PEFC and FSC (page 11), verify the flow of wood from forest to factory to end use, which is essential in ensuring that the timber comes from sustainable sources. Only around 10% of forests are covered by forest certification globally – even though around half of Europe's forests and 40% of North America's are certified. Using wood originating from certified sources or covered by wood origin tracing systems helps to avoid using wood that originates from controversial sources (such as countries where deforestation takes place). Forests are valuable resources and are well looked after in many countries. For example, in Finland the wood industry uses around 50 million m³ of wood, which is less than half of the annual growth of Finnish forests. Around 100 million m³ of wood is added through new growth, so Finnish forests are currently increasing.

Heartwood Northern pine grows slowly in suitable climates to produce close-grained, consistent raw material. The wood is mild textured but strong and straight-grained. It has a large proportion of heartwood. This is the strongest part of the tree: it has excellent strength to weight and is resistant to water and decay.

Each tree has unique growth patterns. Therefore, Finnforest employ sophisticated x-ray and scanning systems to ensure they use each part of the tree as efficiently as possible (pages 60–61).

1

2

3

4

Case Study

Sustainable Forestry in Finland

Featured company Finnforest www.finnforest.com

It takes around three years for a young stand of trees to become well established and they will be at least 60 years old before they are cut down. During this time the trees will be 'thinned' at least twice (image **1**). The thinnings are used as biofuel, pulp (see Pulp, Paper and Board, page 70) or left to rot on the land.

The trees are cut and the location of the harvester can be checked by GPS (image **2**). The wood origin tracing system ensures each piece of wood can be traced to its source. Care is taken to preserve deadwood and retention trees for biodiversity during harvesting and to protect local wildlife. Regulations govern which parts of the forest should be left untouched to safeguard nature – such as areas along streams, banks and anywhere rare species of animals or flora have been discovered.

The wood is sorted as it is cut, collected by a forwarder (image **3**) and transported to the woodyard by water or road (image **4**). Around 70% is used for lumber (page 60) and engineered timber (page 62), and the remaining 30% for paper and board (page 70). Some parts of the tree can be utilized to produce local, renewable energy. Anything that is not used is left to rot on the land.

What is Lumber?

Trees are sawn tangentially or radially to produce lumber. Tangential sawing, known as plain sawn, is the most efficient and economic method for cutting a log (see case study, opposite). Radial cutting, known as quartersawn, produces a more wear-resistant surface finish with an even grain pattern.

The direction of grain affects the strength, working properties and durability of wood. The surface of a plank is typically flat grain: in other words, the plank is cut lengthways from the tree.

Joint designs (page 142) have evolved to maximize the contact of flat grain at an end grain junction. For example, finger joints used to join lengths of timber are designed to maximize flat grain contact and thus improve joint strength.

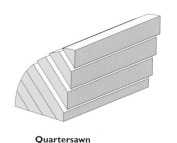
Quartersawn

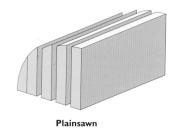
Plainsawn

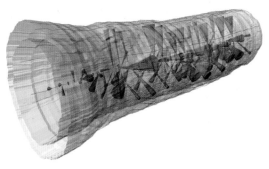

Detailed 3D analysis To ensure the highest quality wood for demanding applications such as external windows, each log is scanned and x-rayed in 3D. This shows up the distance between knots (whorls) and whether they are dead (rotten) or alive (sound), the proportion of heartwood and the annual ring width. This information is used to determine how the log is cut (see opposite).

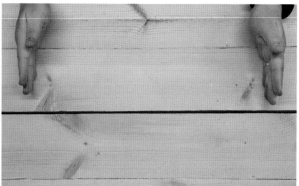

Window frames High quality wooden window frames are produced from lengths of heartwood that have had the knots removed – they can be potential defects. The short parts are finger jointed into continuous lengths of high-strength and durable lumber (see title image, page 56).

1

2

3

Case Study

Sawing Nordic Pine into Lumber

Featured company Finnforest www.finnforest.com

Harvested pine trees are collected from the yard and loaded into the sawmill (image **1**). They are de-barked (image **2**), scanned and x-rayed in 3D. This helps to work out the best way to cut each log, which is determined by computer (image **3**), as they pass through at 50–100 m (164–328 ft) per minute. The logs are cut along their entire length with a band saw (image **4**). The planks are graded and grouped according to quality.

Reducing the moisture content of wood (up to a certain point) is important for many reasons. Drier wood is stronger, stiffer, lighter and less prone to decay than 'green' wood. Traditionally, wood was seasoned in a process known as air-drying at a rate of one year per 25.4 mm (1 in.) to give a final moisture content of 18–20%. Nowadays, modern kiln-drying techniques reduce the moisture content of 25.4 mm (1 in.) thick lumber to under 20% in 10 days (image **5**).

4

5

Engineered Timber

Engineered timber, or lumber, is a composite of wood and adhesive. It includes plywood, laminated veneer lumber (LVL), glue-laminated timber (glulam), oriented strand board (OSB) and I-joists. These materials are strong, dimensionally stable and are very efficient uses of wood for structural and engineering applications.

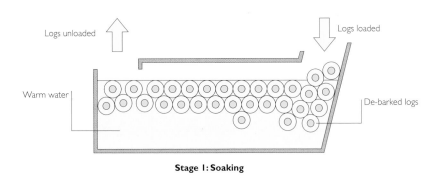

Stage 1: Soaking

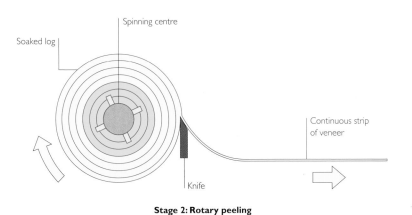

Stage 2: Rotary peeling

Essential Information

AVAILABILITY	●●●●●○○
DURABILITY	●●●●●●●
RECYCLABILITY	●●●●●○○
BIODEGRADABILITY	●●●●○○○

Environmental impacts per kg	
ENERGY	●●○●○○○
RESOURCES	●●●○○○○
POLLUTION	●●○○○○○
WASTE	○○○○○○○

Related materials include:
- Glue-laminated Timber (Glulam)
- I-joists
- Laminated Veneer Lumber (LVL)
- Oriented Strand Board (OSB) and Laminated Strand Lumber (LSL)
- Parallel Strand Lumber (PSL) • Plywood

Alternative and competing materials include:
- Lumber
- Steel and Masonry Construction

What is Rotary Peeling Veneer?

In stage 1, the trees are de-barked and soaked in warm water (50°C/122°F) for 20 hours. This makes the wood more elastic in preparation for the cutting process.

In stage 2, the log is loaded onto rotating centres and a continuous length of veneer is cut from around its circumference using a knife that runs along the entire length. Veneers range from 1 mm to 5 mm (0.04–0.2 in.). The required thickness will depend on the application.

The veneers are dried at 200°C (392°F) in preparation for laminating.

Notes on Environmental Impacts

As with lumber (page 56), wood should be from sustainable and certified forests (see also page 58). Engineered timber has around twice the strength of lumber: there are no weaknesses and it is more consistent and reliable. Therefore, it is used to span longer distances in construction. The Timber Research and Development Association (TRADA) and Lloyds Timber Frame Ltd estimate that a two-storey timber frame house, which also uses wood in the floors and windows, saves 8 tons (17,636 lbs) of carbon dioxide compared to an equivalent masonry house.

The veneers are laminated using phenol formaldehyde (PF) adhesive. Formaldehyde, an industrial chemical, is widely used for glues, paints and textiles. Products that employ formaldehyde must conform to international formaldehyde emissions limits to reduce the negative impact on indoor air quality. Urea formaldehyde (UF) glued products have slightly higher values, but they still fulfil the requirements of the most demanding European standards relating to formaldehyde emission and content.

Waste There is very little waste, if any, from manufacturing timber. By-products, such as sawdust and wood chips, are used as raw materials or biofuel. For example, spruce wood chips are converted into pulp for paper and board production (page 70).

Case Study

Rotary Peeling and Grading Spruce Veneer

Featured company Finnforest www.finnforest.com

Spruce produces dense-ringed, straight-grained, strong and consistent wood. These characteristics make it an ideal material for plywood, LVL and glulam. Birch is durable and strong. It has a higher density than spruce – 750 kg/m³ compared to 500 kg/m³ (46.8 lb/ft³ and 31.2 lb/ft³) – and is used to make plywood (page 68). In both cases the veneer is rotary peeled.

The de-barked logs are lifted from the warm water after soaking for 20 hours (image **1**). The veneer is cut continuously from the log (image **2**). For the production of Finnforest Kerto® LVL, spruce veneer is cut 3 mm (0.12 in.) thick (image **3**). For birch plywood (page 68), however, the veneers are cut 1.4 mm (0.05 in.) thick.

To ensure the highest quality laminate, each sheet of veneer is scanned and the density is measured (image **4**). Pieces with many knots and other defects are separated: the unwanted parts of the sheet are removed and the functional parts stitched together to form usable veneer.

1

3

4

What is Laminated Veneer Lumber?

Laminated veneer lumber (LVL) is produced as a continuous billet. In stage 1, the veneers, which have been coated with PF adhesive, are laid on top of one another. The joints between them are staggered. This ensures that there are no weaknesses in the final material, regardless of where it is cut. The face veneer is selected during rotary peeling (page 63) to ensure the highest quality surface finish.

In stage 2, the veneers are pressed together and heated to 140°C (284°F). This causes the PF to cure and harden, forming a very strong bond between the layers. In stage 3, the billet is cut into 25 m (82 ft) lengths of lumber 2.5 m (8.2 ft) wide. By contrast, sawn lumber is available in lengths up to 6 m × 300 mm (19.7 ft × 11.8 in.).

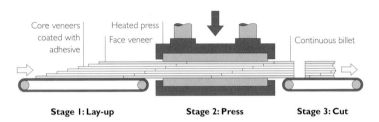

Stage 1: Lay-up   Stage 2: Press   Stage 3: Cut

Metropol Parasol, Seville Designed by Jürgen Mayer H and engineered by Arup, the Metropol Parasol is made from Finnforest Kerto® that has been pressure-treated to protect it outdoors (see also title image, page 62). Construction was completed in March 2011.

Kerto® Ripa Floor cassettes are manufactured off-site to maintain the highest standards and reduce on-site labour. The cassettes are structural (self-supporting) and the insulation is already in situ.

1

Case Study

Producing Kerto® Laminated Veneer Lumber

Featured company Finnforest www.finnforest.com

The pieces of rotary peeled spruce veneer (page 65) are coated with PF adhesive (image **1**). They are laid on top of one another and the joints are staggered (image **2**). In Kerto® S the grain runs in the same direction in all layers (image **3**) unlike in plywood (page 68). In Finnforest Kerto® Q, however, on one layer in every five the grain runs across the width. This is to ensure greater stability for wider panels. The third type of LVL Finnforest produce is Kerto® T, which is the same as S, but the veneers are less dense. This material is used for non-load-bearing applications.

Depending on the number of veneers, the thickness ranges from 27 to 90 mm (1.1–3.5 in.). The lengths of laminated veneers are packed for delivery (image **4**).

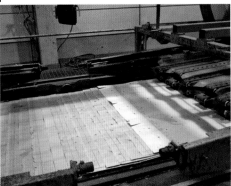

2

3

4

What is Plywood?

Plywood is typically produced from veneers of either birch or spruce, or a mixture of the two, bonded together with PF adhesive. The veneers are laid up cross-banded (grain direction is alternated in each layer). This produces boards that are light, strong, rigid and dimensionally stable.

In stage 1, the veneers, which have been coated with liquid PF adhesive, are pressed together in stacks. The face veneers separate each piece. In stage 2, the veneers are pressed together and heated to 140°C (284°F). This causes the PF to cure and harden, forming a very strong, watertight bond between the layers.

Standard panel thicknesses range from 4 to 50 mm (0.16–1.97 in.).

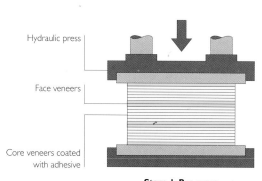

Hydraulic press

Face veneers

Core veneers coated with adhesive

Stage 1: Pre-press

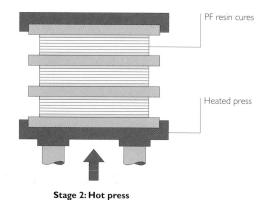

PF resin cures

Heated press

Stage 2: Hot press

Case Study

Birch Plywood

Featured company Finnforest www.finnforest.com

The birch veneers are rotary peeled (page 65), graded and stacked (image **1**). Each stack of veneers will be used for either face or core layers depending on the quality. They are laid up and a thin layer of adhesive is applied between the veneers (image **2**). They are pre-pressed in batches, which are kept apart by the face veneers (image **3**). Each lay-up is then separated and they are hot pressed to fully cure the PF.

The panels are cut and sanded on both sides (image **4**) to produce a high quality, smooth finish.

To improve the durability of plywood a protective film – PF, melamine, thermoplastic or composite – is hot pressed onto the surface (images **5** and **6**). Coated plywood is used for demanding applications, such as construction, weatherproof decking or maintenance-free lorry sidings. For construction, the added protection means the sheet can be reused many times.

1

2

3

4

5

6

Pulp, Paper and Board

Fresh forest fibres are used in the production of paper and board. Compared to recycled pulp, virgin pulp is lighter, stiffer and of known composition. These characteristics make it preferable for applications that demand high performance and clean composition.

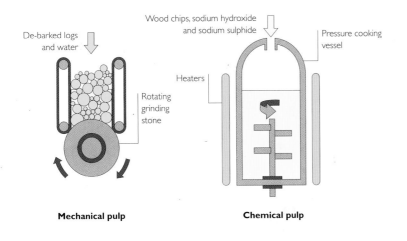

De-barked logs
and water

Rotating
grinding
stone

Mechanical pulp

Wood chips, sodium hydroxide
and sodium sulphide

Pressure cooking
vessel

Heaters

Chemical pulp

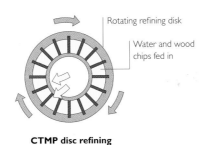

Rotating refining disk

Water and wood
chips fed in

CTMP disc refining

What is Pulping?

Many types of wood are used for pulp, for instance spruce, birch and pine. Spruce and pine produce long fibres, whereas birch provides excellent optical properties. The wood fibres are extracted by mechanical means, chemical processing or chemi-thermo-mechanical pulping (CTMP).

Mechanical grinding converts around 95% of the raw material into pulp. The fibres are extracted by pressing the logs against a rough-surfaced, rotating stone. This produces stiff, short, airy fibres that are less dense than those produced by chemical pulping or CTMP.

In the chemical pulping process, the fibres are extracted by dissolving the lignin with chemicals and heat. This reduces the pulp to around 50% of the raw wood material. Fibres of chemical pulp are flexible and produce a strong network with a large number of strong bonds. They are therefore used in high quality papers and the outside surfaces of packaging board.

CTMP is made from wood chips that have been chemically and thermally softened and then ground in disc refiners. The fibres are more flexible and durable than ground wood pulp and have higher density.

Notes on Environmental Impacts

High quality, lightweight packaging boards consume fewer resources, decrease transportation volumes and produce less waste. In addition, using board with high bending stiffness and compressive strength maintains the quality of the packaging through transportation to the consumer.

Wood pulp must be from sustainably managed forests (see Wood, page 56) to minimize environmental impact. There is virtually no waste in paper and board production. All of the materials are converted into other raw materials or used as biofuel. At the end of their life, pulp products can be recycled (page 212).

Papermaking consumes large quantities of water and bleach; dyes and other chemicals are also used. Metsä Board Corporation reduce their impact on the environment by producing 40% of their energy from biofuel (tree tops, branches and stumps) and using locally sourced wood.

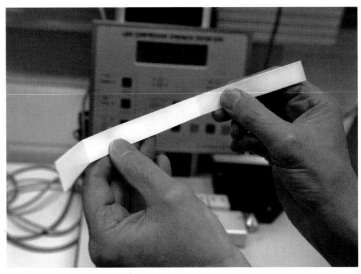

Quality control When the pulp is processed into paper or board the finished sheet is continually tested. Properties such as colour, weight, moisture content and taste are checked and fine adjustments are made to the pulp and production process to ensure the product is of the highest quality.

1

Featured company Metsä Board Corporation
www.metsaboard.com

The most suitable wood for mechanical pulping is spruce. The pulp is used in Metsä Board Corporation packaging board (page 74). Upper parts of the tree and branches (image **1**) that are not suitable for lumber (page 60) or engineered timber (page 62) are converted into pulp.

The logs are cut to length and de-barked by tumbling them with water (image **2**). The waste material is converted into biofuel for the paper mill. The logs pass through a grinder and the pulp is washed and bleached to increase its brightness (image **3**).

2

3

What is Papermaking?

In stage 1, the diluted pulp stock (over 99% water) is dispensed onto a metal mesh which is travelling at speed. This is the forming stage, also known as the 'wet end'. As the water is sucked from the fibre web, draining through the mesh, the fibres remain on the surface and become interwoven. In stage 2, the fibre web is transferred to the press section. Water is squeezed out and absorbed by the press felts between cylinders. High pressure increases fibre bonding and ensures a high-strength and uniform sheet material. In the hot press, stage 3, the water content is reduced from 50% to 7.5% by heated cylinders. In stage 4, the sheet is pressed between polished calendaring rolls to produce a smooth, glossy finish.

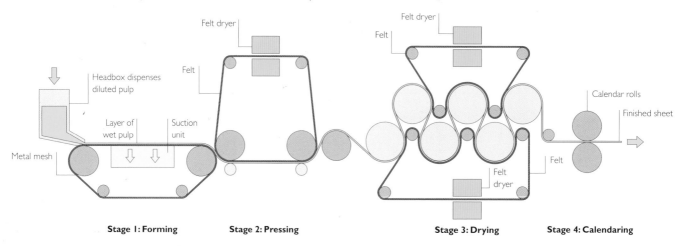

Stage 1: Forming   Stage 2: Pressing   Stage 3: Drying   Stage 4: Calendaring

Case Study

Manufacturing Packaging Board

Featured company Metsä Board Corporation
www.metsaboard.com

Wood pulp is prepared (page 73) and re-pulped with water at the paper mill (image **1**). The fibres are refined and treated to ensure smooth web formation and good fibre bonding. The web makes its way through the wet end, pressing and drying via the series of mesh, felt and rollers (image **2**).

The board is finished with a coating to produce a high quality surface for printing. Ingredients include pigments, binders, additives and water. Clay pigments have a flat profile, which gives the smoothest surface, whereas calcium carbonate particles are round and add brightness. The coating gives the board its final appearance, smoothness, gloss, brightness and absorption characteristics.

The finished board is wound onto jumbo reels (image **3**). These are slit and re-wound based on customer reel orders or sheet orders (image **4**).

1

2

3

4

Leather

Leather is used as a high value material in the fashion, furniture and automotive industries. Tanning is the process of curing rawhides – typically sourced from cows or pigs and a by-product of meat production – into durable leather. It is dyed, embossed and produced in a wide range of finishes.

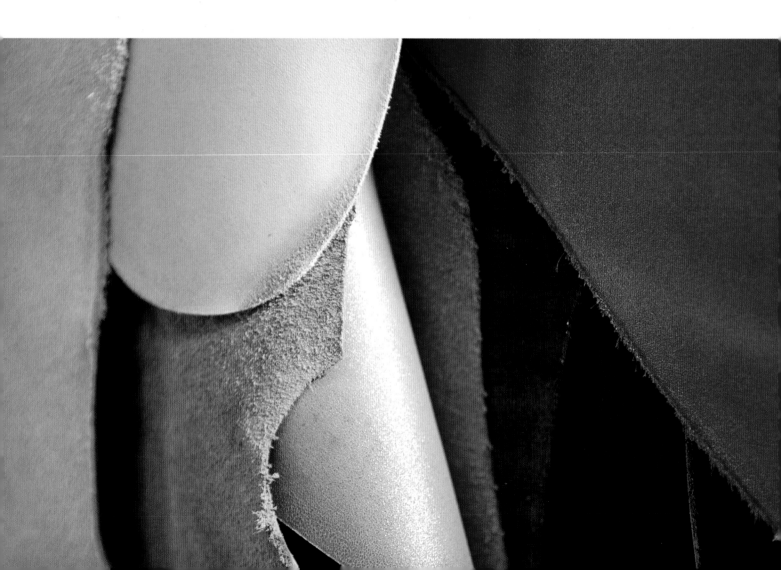

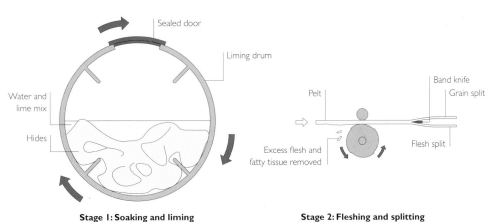

Stage 1: Soaking and liming

Sealed door
Liming drum
Water and lime mix
Hides

Pelt
Band knife
Grain split
Flesh split
Excess flesh and fatty tissue removed

Stage 2: Fleshing and splitting

Essential Information

AVAILABILITY	●	●	●	●	○	○	○
DURABILITY	●	●	●	●	○	○	○
RECYCLABILITY	●	●	●	●	○	○	○
BIODEGRADABILITY	●	●	○	○	○	○	○

Environmental impacts per kg

ENERGY	●	●	●	○	○	○	○
RESOURCES	●	●	○	○	○	○	○
POLLUTION	●	●	●	●	○	○	○
WASTE	●	●	○	○	○	○	○

Related materials include:
• Chrome Tanned Leather   • Vegetable Tanned Leather

What is Soaking and Liming?

Curing animal hides by tanning produces leather. The first stage in the process is soaking and liming.

In stage 1, the rawhides are loaded into the liming drum and soaked in water. Liming takes place in the same drum with the addition of lime and sodium sulphide. This raises the pH value to remove hair. At this stage, substances that cannot be turned into leather, such as natural oils and protein, are removed. After 24 to 36 hours the soaked, limed and de-haired hide, called 'pelt', is removed from the drum.

In stage 2, the pelt is split using a band knife into 'grain split' and 'flesh split'. The grain split will be turned into 'top grain' or 'full grain' (which is the highest quality and is used in jackets, shoes, bags and upholstery, for example) and the flesh split is usually processed into 'split leather' (suede used in bags and upholstery). Lower quality hides that are split and buffed to a smooth finish on the topside are known as 'corrected grain'. They are usually heavily coloured or embossed and are the least expensive.

Notes on Environmental Impacts

Cow and pig hides are those most commonly used for leather goods. The hides are by-products of meat production and are turned into upholstery (page 152), bags, bookbinding, footwear and apparel, for example.

Immediately after slaughter, the skin will start being broken down by bacteria. It is preserved by adding salt (the traditional method used to remove the water) or by refrigeration. The best option is to use locally sourced refrigerated hides because salting can cause pollution, for instance by increasing chloride levels in rivers.

Tanning uses large quantities of water. Heinen Leather uses 90 litres/m² (24 gallons/10 ft²) and around 0.5 kg (1.1 lbs) of chemicals for every 1 kg (2.2 lbs) of leather. However, most tanneries consume more than 350 litres/m² (92.5 gallons/10 ft²). Heinen

Leather purifies all of the water after use. Harmful substances are filtered out, collected and converted. Most of their water can then be reused, which reduces overall water consumption.

The environmental impacts of leather tanning depend on the tannery. Under the Terracare brand, Heinen Leather continuously reduces the amount of water (72% less now than in 2003), chemicals and energy they use (15% of energy is derived from bio-gas that is produced from limed offcuts). In doing so, they are a key player in reducing the environmental impact of leather production. As a result, it is estimated that the production of 1 m² (10ft²) of their leather results in 2.81 kg (6.19 lbs) of carbon dioxide equivalent emissions.

Case Study

Preparing Rawhides for Tanning

Featured company Heinen Leather
www.heinen-leather.de

Heinen Leather is based in Germany and uses only locally sourced (Central European) refrigerated cowhide. They buy bull hide weighing 30–50 kg (66–110 lbs) or up to 60 kg (132 lbs) for its heaviest leather, which arrives graded and sorted (image **1**).

They are soaked and limed in batches (image **2**) and the pelt is mechanically de-fleshed and trimmed. Unwanted parts of the hide, such as the kneecaps and root of the tail, are cut off (image **3**). There is no waste from the hide. All unwanted parts are put to other uses, such as the production of glue or gelatin.

The pelt is cut through its thickness into grain and flesh split (images **4** and **5**) and is ready for tanning (page 80).

I

2

3

4

5

What is Chrome Tanning?

Tanning cures the leather to make it durable and resistant to water. Two principal methods of tanning are vegetable and mineral (chrome). Vegetable tanning uses tannin obtained from biomass such as tree bark (this is where the name originates from). Traditional methods take about one year and produce firm and hard-wearing leather, although the leather will not be as long lasting as chrome-tanned leather. The pelts are suspended in tanning pits and moved through a cycle of progressively stronger concentrations of tannin solution, which is known as 'liquor'.

Chrome tanning is more widely used, faster (it takes around 20 hours) and produces consistent and high quality leather. Stage 1 consists of five processes, which are carried out in sequence in a rotating drum: de-liming, bating, pickling, tanning and basification (see case study, opposite).

In stage 2, the water is pressed out on a sammying machine and the hides are cut down the middle, which makes them easier to handle.

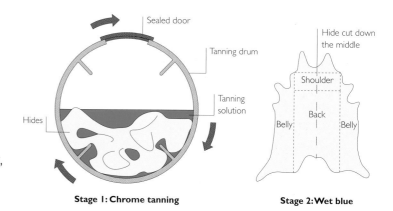

Stage 1: Chrome tanning

Sealed door
Tanning drum
Tanning solution
Hides

Stage 2: Wet blue

Hide cut down the middle
Shoulder
Back
Belly
Belly

Chromium salts Many different types of tanning agent can be used. Trivalent chromium (chromium III), which is used by Heinen Leather, is a natural, non-toxic element thought to have the least environmental impact of all tanning agents. Hexavalent chromium (chromium VI) is banned in many countries, including Germany, because it is known to be carcinogenic.

1

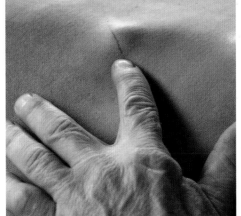

2

3

4

5

Featured company Heinen Leather
www.heinen-leather.de

Heinen Leather uses carbon dioxide to de-lime the pelts. Collagen and other proteins are then removed by using enzymes in a process known as 'bating'. This makes the fibres more pliable. During pickling, salt and acid are added to reduce the pH and make the leather ready for the addition of the tanning agent. At low pH the chromium molecules are very small and so penetrate deep into the leather fibres. As the pH rises the molecules grow and form cross-links with the collagen. This act of curing is the tanning process.

The tanned hides are known as 'wet blue' because the chromium dyes them a light shade of blue (image 1). Hide flaws, such as scratches and scars, are easily identified on the wet blue leathers (image 2). The graders, known as 'wet blue classifiers', carefully sort the leather into the different classes of quality (image 3).

The hides are shaved to the correct thickness, which depends on the application (images 4 and 5). Soft leather for bags, for example, requires a different thickness from walking boots.

What is Retanning and Dyeing?

The shaved leathers are loaded into the dyeing drum and go through a process of neutralization, retanning, dyeing and greasing. Additional tanning agents are added to influence softness, feel, tearing value, elasticity and other characteristics. Dye is added to obtain the desired colour and the pigments are mixed according to each batch of leather.

Skin grease, which was removed during liming, is added to improve the colour, lustre and feel of the leather. Hydrophobic greases improve the leather's resistance to water absorption. The breathability of the leather is maintained because the grease wraps around the individual fibres.

After dyeing the leather is dried in the sammying machine. The grain side (underside) is made smoother and more even by a 'setting-out' cylinder with blunt blades.

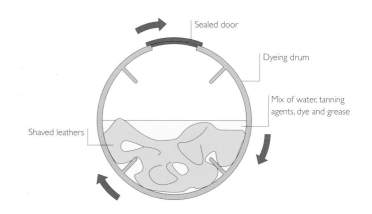

Sealed door

Dyeing drum

Mix of water, tanning agents, dye and grease

Shaved leathers

Finishing The leather is ironed at around 90°C (194°F) and stretched slightly to improve surface finish. Once trimmed it is known as 'crust leather' and is ready to use. A wide range of finishes is available: for instance, buffing on the front side to produce a roughened, more hard-wearing surface (nubuck); dry-splitting to a precise thickness accurate to 0.1 mm (0.004 in.); softening by tumbling in the milling drum to produce a velvety feel (such as nappa); spraying or roll coating (colour, metallic effect, wax, lacquer and so on); embossing (such as grain pattern) or printing (colour and pattern).

1

2

3

4

Case Study

Dyeing, Drying and Finishing Leather

Featured company Heinen Leather
www.heinen-leather.de

During this stage the leather is given specific qualities relevant to the customer's requirements. Each batch is processed separately (image **1**). A wide range of chemicals is used for dyeing and finishing (image **2**). Heinen Leather use only water-based products.

After dyeing, the leather is placed grain-side down onto a heated metal plate (40°C/104°F) (image **3**). With the addition of vacuum pressure, the leather is dried (but not completely) and the fibres are 'fixed' in place.

The leathers are hung to complete the drying process slowly (image **4**). This allows the chemicals added to the leather to form strong bonds and produce a stable and high quality material. At Heinen Leather the heat used in this process is taken from waste generated from other processes. After drying the leather is softened with water and vibrating metal pins (staking) to make softer leather with improved surface finish (image **5**). It is now ready for one of many finishing processes (see image, opposite).

5

Wool

This natural and renewable material is harvested annually from sheep around the world. Depending on the breed and country of origin, the quality ranges from coarse and resilient to fine and comfortable. This makes it suitable for a wide range of applications including clothing, upholstery and technical textiles.

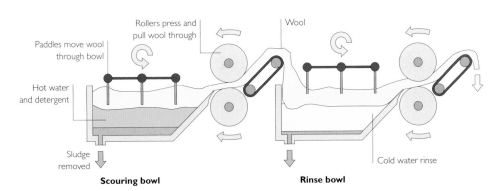

Paddles move wool
through bowl

Hot water
and detergent

Rollers press and
pull wool through

Wool

Sludge
removed

Scouring bowl

Cold water rinse

Rinse bowl

Essential Information

AVAILABILITY	●●●●●●○
DURABILITY	●●●●●●○
RECYCLABILITY	●●●○○○○
BIODEGRADABILITY	●●●●●○○

Environmental impacts per kg

ENERGY	●●○○○○○
RESOURCES	●○○○○○○
POLLUTION	●●●○○○○
WASTE	●●●○○○○

Related materials include:
- Carded
- Fabric
- Worsted Yarn
- Dyed
- Woollen Yarn

Alternative and competing materials include:
- Synthetic Fibre

What is Wool Scouring?

The conversion of 'greasy wool' to 'wool top' (finished wool) consists of scouring, carding and combing. Collectively, this is called topmaking.

Scouring is the process of removing all the sweat, grease, dirt and other contamination that has built up on the fleece over the course of a year. Aqueous scouring involves passing the fleece through six to eight tanks (bowls), starting with hot water (60°C/140°F) mixed with detergent and finishing with a clean rinse. At each stage the wool is cleaned and the contamination removed.

Rollers between the tanks pull the wool through and apply pressure, squeezing the dirty water out, which reduces the contamination between bowls.

Wool grease is extracted from the remaining sludge and refined into lanolin, which is an important ingredient in the cosmetic and pharmaceutical industries.

Notes on Environmental Impacts

Wool is a natural material with many advantageous properties. It is water-resistant, fire-resistant (it will burn in a flame, but self-extinguish when no longer in it), a good insulator (it traps air), absorbs water without feeling wet and dyes well.

Production of wool fibres, including scouring – which requires 4 litres (1 gallon) of water per 1 kg (2.2 lbs) of wool – has a lower environmental impact than the production of synthetic fibres such as polypropylene (PP) or polyamide (PA) nylon.

Each stage in the wool production process is being made more efficient and the environmental impact reduced. For example, Haworth Scouring are certified by the Soil Association and their processes are organic. Even so, the production of wool requires that sheep are reared on farms, and protected with medicine and pesticides, while harmful chemicals are used in the production of the yarn, and in some countries animal welfare is an issue.

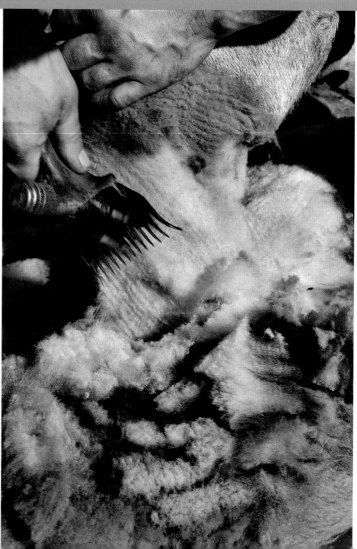

Sheep shearing A shepherd – here, Gareth J. Daniels – shears the sheep each summer. It is physical work and must be done well to ensure the least stress to the sheep and to maintain highest quality fleece. For example, taking two passes with the clippers instead of one will result in shorter fibres, known as second cuts, that are not desirable for spinning high quality yarn (page 91).

1

2

3

Grading and Scouring Wool

Featured company British Wool Marketing Board
www.britishwool.org.uk and Haworth Scouring
www.haworthscouring.co.uk

Wool grows from follicles in the sheep's skin with a wavy structure, known as crimp (image **1**). It grows in clumps called staples. They are pulled from the fleece to check the quality (image **2**), in particular the strength, length and diameter of the fibre and the consistency of the crimp. These qualities, along with breed and colour, are used to grade the wool. In the UK the British Wool Marketing Board collects, grades and sells all wool.

The wool is blended and 'opened up' (image **3**) to prepare it for scouring (image **4**). There is significant contamination in wool that has to be removed: 1,000 tons (2,205,000 lbs) of fleece produces around 700 tons (1,543,000 lbs) of washed, clean wool (image **5**).

4

5

What is Carding?

Wool fibres are proteins and their outer surface is covered with tiny overlapping scales, which help the fibres to grip together. Carding blends and aligns the fibres into a more even web, which is then converted into either woollen yarn (tangled fibres of mixed length) or worsted yarn (combed long, parallel fibres).

The rotating worker rollers pick up wool that has not yet been straightened (lying across the direction of travel), from the swift roller. In turn, the fibres are picked from the worker rollers by counter-rotating stripper rollers, which return them to the swift roller. In this way, the wool fibres are gradually separated, blended and distributed to form an even mix.

The fancy roller is covered with wire hooks that brush against the swift, lifting the fibres and easing transition to the doffer roller. Not all fibres are transferred and so the remainder continue on the swift and the cycle continues. The fine fibrous web is drawn away from the doffer by a fly comb, which jigs up and down rapidly. The web is separated into strips by taut tapes and gently twisted (the size is defined by the application).

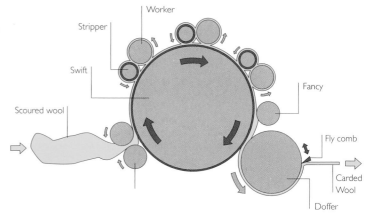

Case Study

Carded Wool

Featured company Haworth Scouring
www.haworthscouring.co.uk

After scouring the wool is clean, but the fibres are tangled and there is still some vegetable matter that has to be removed (image **1**). The bundles of wool are loaded into the carding machine (image **2**).

The large swift roller rotates in the middle. It is surrounded by a combination of slow-moving worker rollers and smaller stripper rollers (image **3**). The workers rotate relatively slowly, so that the fibres do not return to the same place on the swift roller with each rotation. In this way the wool is blended and evenly distributed.

The fibres are transferred from the swift to the doffer and removed as a continuous fibrous web (image **4**), which is lightly twisted into slivers that are stored in drums (image **5**). The mixed fibres (image **6**) can be converted directly into woollen yarn by twisting (light, airy yarn suitable for weaving, knitwear or felt-making). Alternatively, the slivers are gilled (thinned out), combed (to remove short fibres and align the long fibres) and twisted into a

1

strong, hard yarn, known as worsted (see also blending, dyeing and weaving, page 90).

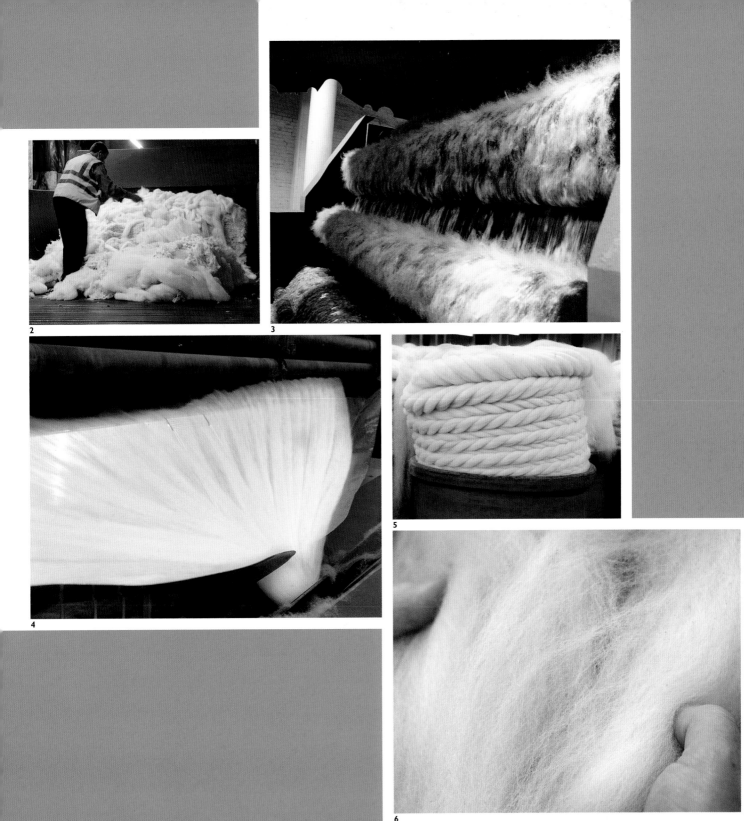

2

3

4

5

6

Case Study

Dyeing and Colour Blending

Featured company Mallalieu's of Delph
www.mallalieus.com

The clean wool is dyed in large vats of boiling water (image **1**). Dyes contain many different ingredients and great effort has been made to make sure they are safe and purely a colouring agent. Declarations for health and safety and tests on cloth before it goes into apparel are necessary to avoid any incidents arising from manufacture or use. The wool is hoisted in large bags (image **2**), which are used to transfer it to the hydroextraction and radio frequency drying processes.

The wool is blended in a Fearnought machine, which breaks down the clumps through counter-rotating action (images **3** and **4**). Various shades of colour are mixed to create a rich colour in application. The fibres pass through a synthetic oiling unit to reduce dryness and are deposited into a hopper (image **5**).

1

2

3

4

5

Case Study

Carding and Spinning

Featured company Mallalieu's of Delph
www.mallalieus.com

The blended wool, which in this case
is brown, is passed through a five-stage
carding process (page 88). In between
each swift, the wool is realigned against the
direction of travel to ensure the colour is
fully mixed. Gradually the wool is reduced
to a very fine fibrous web, which is
separated by leather belts (image **1**).
The fibres are rolled into loosely twisted
yarns taken up on spools (images **2** and **3**).

The threads are drawn through a
rotating tube (image **4**), which applies
additional twist to produce a stronger
thread (image **5**) less prone to breakage.

1

4

5

What is Loom Weaving?

Loom weaving consists of three movements repeated many times: raising and lowering the heddle bars, feeding the weft and beating.

Each strand of warp is fed through an eyelet in the heddle bar. The heddle bars are operated individually – or as a set – and are computer-guided or moved by depressing a foot pedal. Moving them up and down determines whether the warp or weft will be visible from the top side. This is how patterns, which can be very intricate, are made. In the example in the diagram the heddles are separated into two sets, which creates a plain or basket weave.

A weft is fed into the space between the fibres and in front of the beater. The beater is a series of blunt blades that sit between each fibre. They are used to 'beat' each weft tightly into the overlapping warp.

The weft is held in place by the beater while the lower heddle bar moves up and the upper heddle bar moves down to lock the weft between the warps. The process is repeated to form the next run.

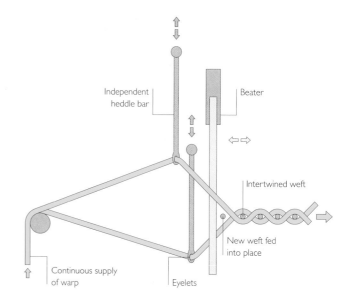

Independent heddle bar

Beater

Intertwined weft

New weft fed into place

Continuous supply of warp

Eyelets

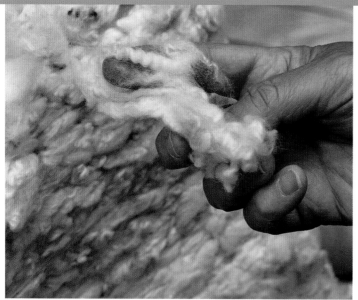

Wool quality Wool is selected according to the weaving requirements. The wool from each breed of sheep has its own characteristics, including colour, durability, density, fibre size, crimp and lustre. For example, British wool is hard-wearing and resilient and so mostly used for carpets (70%), whereas wool from Australia and New Zealand is considered more comfortable and suitable for knitwear.

1

2

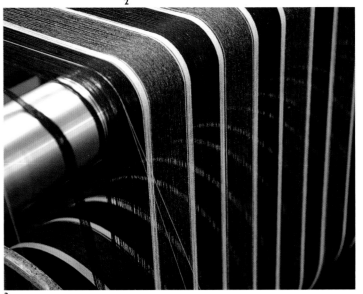

3

Case Study

Weaving a Patterned Fabric

Featured company Mallalieu's of Delph
www.mallalieus.com

In preparation for weaving, the wool must be dyed and blended (page 90), carded and spun into yarn (page 88). The ringspun thread (image **1**) is then transferred onto cones and onto a balloon cylinder, which will form the basis of the pattern to be woven. From the balloon cylinder the warp yarn is transferred to a beam (image **2**). The beam is, in turn, transferred to the loom after some initial preparation (image **3**). Each thread is passed through an eyelet in the heddle bar, which moves up and down to intertwine the weft threads that run perpendicular to the warp. The most common weaves are plain, twill and satin. With these techniques an almost unlimited range of colours and patterns can be created. After each weft thread has passed between the layers of warp, a beater compresses the threads into a tight weave (image **4**).

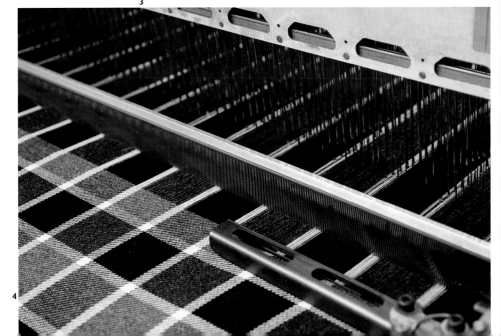

4

Plant Fibres

Used to make high quality and technical textiles for fashion, packaging, upholstery and biocomposites, vegetable cellulosic fibres are natural, renewable and strong. The methods of farming and production are critical to ensuring a positive environmental impact.

Cotton

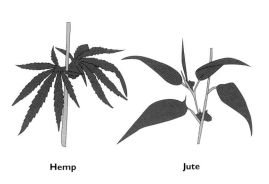

Hemp　　　　　**Jute**　　　　　**Flax**

Bast fibres

Essential Information

AVAILABILITY	●●●●●●○
DURABILITY	●●●●●●○
RECYCLABILITY	●●●●●○○
BIODEGRADABILITY	●●●●●●●

Environmental impacts per kg	
ENERGY	●○●●●●●
RESOURCES	●●●●○○○
POLLUTION	●●●○●●●
WASTE	●●○●●●●

Related materials include:
- Cotton
- Hemp
- Flax
- Jute

Alternative and competing materials include:
- Cellulose Acetate (CA)
- Virgin Plastic (Synthetic Fibres)

What are Plant Fibres?

Plant fibres, also referred to as vegetable fibres, are comprised mainly of cellulose and derived from the seeds or stems (bast) of cultivated crops. Hemp is fast growing, has high yield and produces soft, long, durable fibres. Flax fibres are equally durable, long, soft and flexible and it is becoming increasingly popular because the fibres are thinner and easier to separate than hemp. Jute produces a coarse and strong fibre that is less expensive, but is not grown in Europe. It is commonly used to make durable hessian cloth for carpets, bags and sacks. Bast fibre extraction starts with retting. Chemical-free processes are effective and produce a superior and sustainable fibre.

The most widely used fibre comes from the cottonseed pod. The soft and light staple fibres attached to the seedpod are spun into yarn. The seedpod, also known as boll, contains shorter fibres that are used in papermaking (page 74) and cellulose acetate (page 30). The fibres are separated by mechanical means.

Notes on Environmental Impacts

The combination of fibre type (growing) and production method (fibre extraction) determines the overall environmental impact. Cotton is one of the most heavily sprayed field crops (it accounts for more than 10% of agro-chemical consumption). Organic cotton, which is grown without chemical fertilisers, pesticides and fungicides, is more sustainable.

By contrast, plants that yield bast fibres can be grown with little or no fungicide, herbicide or pesticides in many climates.

Bamboo is emerging as a cost-effective alternative to silk. It is fast growing and does not require fungicide, herbicide or pesticides. However, it should be noted that bamboo viscous fibre is not considered a natural plant fibre due to the chemical processes used to produce the fibres. The dominant method is by hydrolysis alkalization with multiple bleaching phases. Chemicals, such as sodium hydroxide (caustic soda), are used to extract the cellulose, which is then extruded into a fibre. Mechanical methods have lower environmental impact, but with current technology fibre quality is inferior.

With all plant fibres, as for wood (page 56), certification is key to monitoring the overall impact of the production processes (page 10).

Case Study

Growing and Harvesting Flax

Featured company EKOTEX
www.ekotex.com.pl

Flax is harvested and the stalks are laid down in the field to ret (image **1**). Retting is a natural process, whereby micro-organisms dissolve the pectin that binds the fibres to the stem and each other. After four to six weeks the dry stalks are baled and delivered to the scutching mill (image **2**) where the stalks are pressed between metal rolls to separate the fibres mechanically. The fibres are combed and carded (image **3**), much like wool (page 84).

1

2

3

Case Study

Converting Flax into Biotex Composite

Featured company Composites Evolution
www.compositesevolution.com

Carding produces a sliver of fibres (image **1**). 'Twistless' spinning of the yarn was developed for the production of composites, helping to maintain the highest performance with continuous fibre reinforcement. It is best to use the fibre untreated if possible – this is known as 'natural' – to avoid the use of bleaching and dyeing chemicals. If not, water-based systems without heavy metals or other toxic ingredients are available (see image, page 10). A range of different weaves is produced: they are tailored to the mechanical requirements of the application (image **2**).

Composites Evolution use flax to manufacture Biotex, a range of high performance natural composites (see Biocomposite Prepreg, page 98). This technology is used to make parts for the Lola/Drayson racing Le Mans prototype electric car (page 129) and WorldFirst racing car (page 13) sponsored by Warwick Innovative Manufacturing Research Centre (WIMRC) at Warwick Manufacturing Group.

This prototype interior panel for Land Rover (image **3**), made from Biotex Flax/ polypropylene (PP), is 60% lighter than the current steel part at the same stiffness. Composites Evolution also supply a material with polylactic acid (PLA) to produce 100% biocomposite.

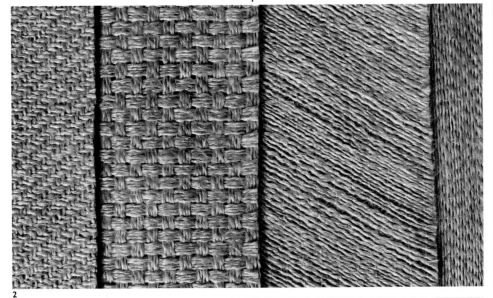

2

3

Biocomposite Prepreg

Natural fibres, such as hemp, flax and jute, are being used to reinforce composites for the automotive industry to reduce weight, cost and environmental impact. They are replacing conventional composites, such as glass-filled plastics and sheet metal, for both structural and decorative applications.

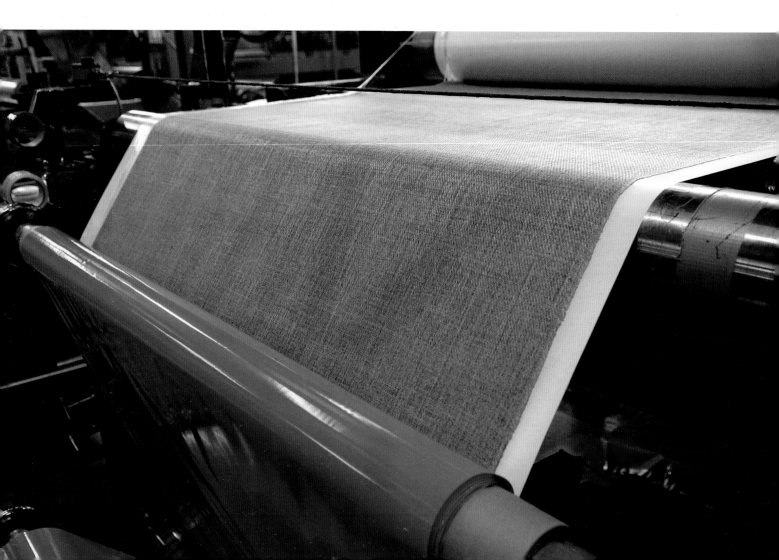

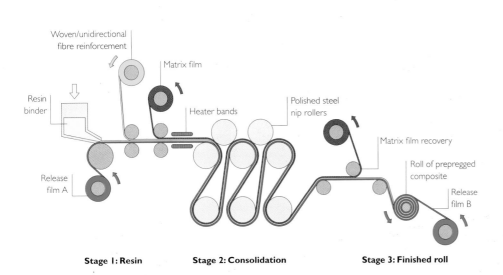

Woven/unidirectional
fibre reinforcement

Matrix film

Resin
binder

Heater bands

Polished steel
nip rollers

Matrix film recovery

Roll of prepregged
composite

Release
film A

Release
film B

Stage 1: Resin   **Stage 2: Consolidation**   **Stage 3: Finished roll**

Essential Information

AVAILABILITY	●●●●●●○
DURABILITY	●●●●●●●
RECYCLABILITY	●●○○○○○
BIODEGRADABILITY	●●●●●○○

Environmental impacts per kg	
ENERGY	●●○○○○○
RESOURCES	●●○○○○○
POLLUTION	●●●○○○○
WASTE	●●●●○○○

Alternative and competing materials include:
- Plastic   • Recycled Plastic
- Steel

What is Hot-melt Prepreg?

Pre-impregnating with resin, which is known as prepregging, is the process of combining a resin matrix with continuous fibre reinforcement for applications in composite laminating (page 126) or compression molding (page 110). The matrix supports and bonds the fibres, transferring applied loads and protecting the fibres from damage. It also governs the maximum service temperature of a composite. Thermoplastics (page 22), thermosets and bioplastics (page 24) are all suitable matrices.

In stage 1, an exact measure of resin is applied to the release film A, ensuring a controlled resin to fibre ratio.

The fibre reinforcement is laid on top, locked in by the matrix film and compressed. Types of fibre reinforcement include woven, unidirectional (all fibres in one direction) and non-crimp/multi-axial fabrics.

In stage 2, the laminate passes through a series of polished steel nip rollers, which force the resin into the reinforcement. In stage 3, the backing substrate carrying the resin film is removed and the prepregged composite is wound onto a roll with release film B on the topside.

Notes on Environmental Impacts

The most important factors affecting the total environmental impact of composites are the ingredients and end-of-life. Conventional composites, such as carbon, glass and aramid fibre-reinforced plastic (CFRP, GFRP and AFRP), are very light, stiff and strong. They are changing the way high performance products are designed and built, improving efficiency and enabling structures that would otherwise be impractical. However, carbon and aramid (also known under the trade names Kevlar® and Twaron®) are very energy intensive to produce and at the end of their life composites are very complex to recycle (although there has been significant development in this area: see image, page 17).

Biocomposites are made up of natural fibre reinforcement (see Plant Fibres, page 94) and bioplastic (page 24), also called bioresin. Alternatively, they are bio-based and consist of a synthetic resin matrix or non-bio fibre reinforcement. Thermoplastics (page 22) are highly recyclable, whereas thermosets are less easily recycled. Bio ingredients require less energy to manufacture than synthetic equivalents (see Bio-based Plastics, page 24). The recyclability has also been studied: flax/polylactic acid (PLA) laminates were shredded, regranulated, injection molded (page 104) and tensile tested – this cycle was performed five times. The strength of the recycled material reduced by 10% with each round of recycling, but the modulus was unaffected. Flax/PLA is also biodegradable and compostable in the right conditions.

Biocomposite prototype for Jaguar A prototype part by Composites Evolution made up of woven flax and PLA (page 97) Biotex. This Jaguar XF rear door module is 35% lighter than the current glass-filled (GF) polypropylene (PP) component of the same thickness.

1

2

3

4

Case Study

Preparing Flax Fibre Composite

Featured company Umeco www.umeco.co.uk and
Composites Evolution www.compositesevolution.com

This is the production of flax-epoxy bio-based composite. Several different types of weave can be used including plain, twill and satin. Plain fabric (one over, one under) is very stable, but difficult to drape around sharp profile changes. Using a heavy balance of fibres in the warp direction produces a near unidirectional format. Twill fabrics (two over, two under to create a diagonal pattern) have an open weave, readily draping and conforming to complex profiles. Satin weave (four over, one under, for example) is a much flatter fabric that can be easily draped to a complex surface profile. However, due to this construction, such weaves are unbalanced.

In this case, the fibre reinforcement is twill flax (image **1**). Similar to hemp, flax has good mechanical properties and can be grown in a European climate, near to the factory. It is passed through the hot-melt process, consolidated with resin and taken up on a roll in between release films (images **2** and **3**). The process is carefully controlled to ensure the highest quality material (image **4**). This is essential because these materials are used in demanding applications where predictable mechanical performance is critical.

Processes

2

Injection Molding Bioplastic

Bioplastics are used as a direct replacement for conventional petroleum-based plastics in this versatile mass production process. There are many types of bio ingredients that are used at different concentration levels, from a small amount to 100%, depending on the requirements of the application.

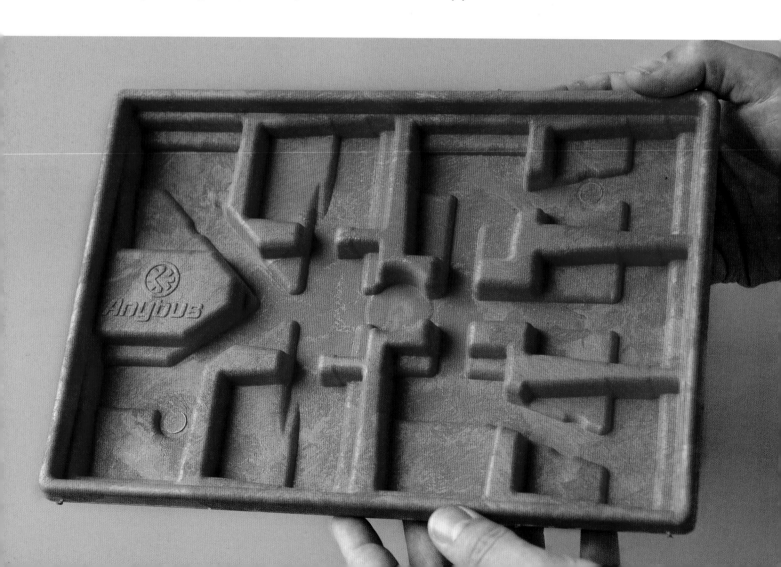

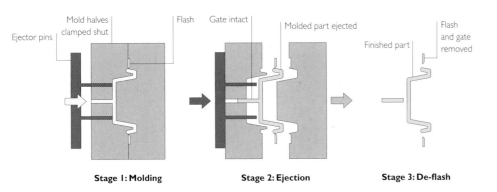

Ejector pins | Mold halves clamped shut | Flash | Gate intact | Molded part ejected | Flash and gate removed | Finished part

Stage 1: Molding   **Stage 2: Ejection**   **Stage 3: De-flash**

Essential Information

VISUAL QUALITY	●●●●●●○
SPEED	●●●●●●○
SET-UP COST	●●●●●●○
UNIT COST	●●○○○○○

Environmental impacts per kg	
ENERGY	●●○○○○○○
RESOURCES	●●○○○○○○
POLLUTION	●○○○○○○○
WASTE	●○○○○○○○

Alternative and competing processes include:

- Blow Molding
- Die Cutting and Carton Construction
- Compression Molding
- Thermoforming

What is Injection Molding Starch-based Plastic?

PaperFoam is made up of 70% starch, 15% fibres and 15% premix (secret ingredient) (see Bio-based plastics, page 24). In stage 1, the mixed material is injected through the gate into the die cavity under pressure. The mold is operated at 200°C (392°F), so that the water boils as the material is injected into the cavity. This causes the material to foam.

In stage 2, after 60 to 90 seconds and once all the water has vaporized, the molded part is ejected. In stage 3, the flash and gate are removed for recycling. The molds are generally machined from aluminium.

Notes for Designers

QUALITY The high pressure ensures good repeatability. However, the type of material will determine the finish and quality. For example, starch-based plastics have a mottled appearance whereas polylactic acid (PLA) and polyhydroxyalkanoate (PHA) have a similar appearance to conventional plastics (see Biodegradable Plastic image, page 22).

TYPICAL APPLICATIONS Applications depend on the type of bioplastic: starch-based plastics are used for packaging, loose fill, bottles, caps, cutlery, food boxes and cups; wood-based plastics are used for disposable items, packaging, handles and toys; and PLA and PHA are used as a direct replacement for petroleum-based plastic in packaging, cutlery, textiles and agricultural applications.

COST AND SPEED Set-up costs are moderate depending on the size and complexity of the part. Cycle time is generally between 30 and 90 seconds, and labour costs are low for mechanized operations. The bioplastic unit price will generally be higher than commodity plastics. Volumes are typically above 25,000.

MATERIALS All types of plastic can be molded, including starch-based, wood-based, PLA, PHA and poly-beta-hydroxybutyrate (PHB), and cellulose-based, as well as conventional thermoplastics (page 20). It is also possible to mold rubber (page 36).

ENVIRONMENTAL IMPACTS Bio-based materials are derived from renewable sources. This uses 20% to 30% less energy and results in up to 85% lower carbon emissions than in the production of petroleum-based plastics. They can be compostable or biodegradable, which means they are broken down into carbon dioxide, water and biomass by micro-organisms.

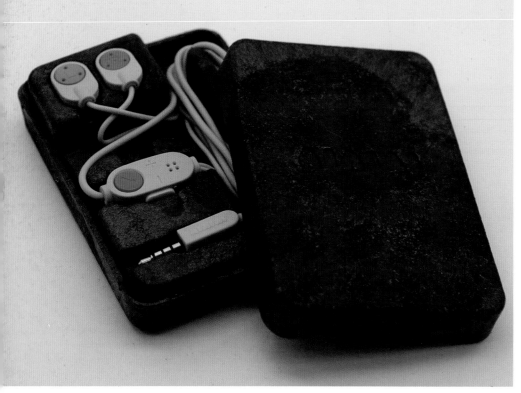

Packaging This material is used in all types of packaging applications, from disposable food packaging to delicate electronics goods. PaperFoam is tested to the same standards as conventional packaging materials. Wall thickness can be 2–3.5 mm (0.08–0.14 in.) and sizes range from roughly 50 mm (2 in.) in diameter to 300 x 200 x 100 mm (12 x 8 x 4 in.).

1

2

3

Case Study

Injection Molding Starch-based Plastic

Featured company PaperFoam www.paperfoam.com

The raw material used in PaperFoam molding is prepared using similar equipment to food production (page 25). It has a sticky consistency and the natural colour is off-white (image **1**). It is available in a range of colours (see page 24).

The tools are machined from aluminium and in this case three parts are molded simultaneously (image **2**). The mold is clamped shut, the bioplastic injected and solidified. After only 70 to 90 seconds the mold halves separate to reveal the formed parts (image **3**).

The parts are ejected and flash is removed by a robot or by hand (image **4**). The packaging is designed to stack neatly and save space during shipping (image **5**).

4

5

Wood-based plastic screw used in S-HOUSE

Treeplast® is employed in complex molding, such as this screw, which is 365 mm (14.4 in.) in length. It is used in the construction of S-HOUSE to hold together straw bales (GrAT www.grat.tuwien.ac.at).

Case Study

Injection Molding Wood-based Plastic

Featured company Treeplast www.treeplast.com

Treeplast® is a bio-based renewable material that can be injection molded. The exact ingredients vary according to the application and include wood chips, crushed corn and bioplastic matrix. In this case, the bioplastic is polyhydroxybutyrate (PHB). It is a polyester – a type of polyhydroxyalkanoate (PHA) (page 106) with similar strength to polypropylene (PP) – produced by bacterial fermentation.

The properties of PHA polyesters range from stiff to elastic and biodegradable to long lasting, depending on the monomers used in polymerization (page 21). The production of PHA uses less energy than petroleum-based plastic.

The granules of pre-mixed material (image **1**) are produced by extrusion and formed with conventional molding equipment (image **2**). It is viscous compared to pure plastic and so will require higher molding pressures and thicker wall sections. As a result, the maximum size that can be injection molded is around 450 x 250 x 250 mm

(17.7 x 9.8 x 9.8 in.) and the minimum dimensions are around 3 x 3 x 3 mm (0.1 x 0.1 x 0.1 in.).

The visual quality of the part is heavily influenced by the bio content (image **3**). As in conventional plastic molding, flash is removed and the parts are finished (image **4**).

1

2

3

4

Compression Molding

Compression molding is used to form rubber, bioplastic, composite and recycled materials into 3D parts with a simple two-part mold. It is mainly utilized for batch production or to shape materials that are not suitable for injection molding.

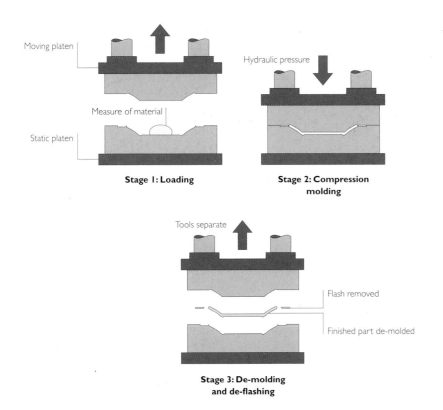

Moving platen

Measure of material

Static platen

Stage 1: Loading

Hydraulic pressure

Stage 2: Compression molding

Tools separate

Flash removed

Finished part de-molded

Stage 3: De-molding and de-flashing

Essential Information

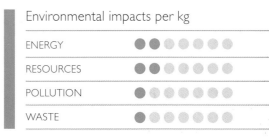

VISUAL QUALITY	●●●●●●○○
SPEED	●●●●○○○○
SET-UP COST	●●●●●○○○
UNIT COST	●●●●○○○○

Environmental impacts per kg	
ENERGY	●●○○○○○○
RESOURCES	●●○○○○○○
POLLUTION	●○○○○○○○
WASTE	●○○○○○○○

Alternative and competing processes include:
- Injection Molding
- Thermoforming

What is Compression Molding?

Compression molding is generally carried out using a simple two-part mold. Undercuts are possible with side action in the mold, but this is limited by material selection.

In stage 1, a predetermined quantity of material is loaded into the lower, static mold. The molds are pre-heated: the temperature is determined by the material being formed. In stage 2, the two halves of the mold are brought together and pressure is applied gradually to encourage the material to flow. Flash traps allow excess material to escape in a controlled manner. They are designed so that the flash can be easily detached after molding.

In stage 3, the part is de-molded and de-flashed once it has fully solidified.

QUALITY The choice of material determines the visual and mechanical properties of the finished part. For example, starch-based plastics have a mottled surface appearance, whereas recycled plastics can be multi-coloured (see recycled plastic sheet molding, page 124).

TYPICAL APPLICATIONS Compression molding is utilized in a wide variety of products such as shoe soles, wellington boots, grommets, utensil handles, packaging and sheet materials.

COST AND SPEED Tooling costs are low to moderate (less than for injection molding). Cycle time depends on size, material and thickness. The process is suitable for low-volume to mass production, but injection molding (page 104) is usually preferred for mass production because it is more cost effective for high volumes, although this depends on the material. Labour costs are low.

MATERIALS Natural materials include agricultural by-products, starch-based plastic and cellulose-based plastic. Almost any type of material can be incorporated with the molding material: for example, fibres.

ENVIRONMENTAL IMPACTS Plant materials are harvested from renewable sources, are locally produced or are by-products of agricultural processes. Nothing is added during molding – heat is required and in some cases a mold release agent is used – and there is little or no waste.

Molded and bonded rubber boots GreenTips wellington boots are made in Sri Lanka and contain only fairtrade natural rubber (page 36) certified by the Forest Stewardship Council (FSC). This means the rubber used to make the boots contains no added chemicals, polyvinyl chloride (PVC) or toxins, and was tapped from a tree in a sustainable manner (page 38), which prevents deforestation or displacement of indigenous people or wildlife.

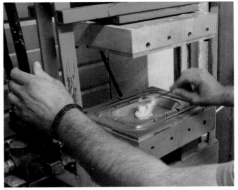

Case Study

Molding a Starch-based Plastic Tray

Featured company PaperFoam www.paperfoam.com

In this case, PaperFoam are using compression molding to test mixes of material prior to full production, which will utilize injection molding (page 104). The starch, water, wood fibres and 'premix' proprietary ingredient are combined in a food mixer (image **1**). This demonstrates how close to food making this particular bioplastic process can be.

An exact measure of material is placed into the lower mold (image **2**). The molds are preheated to 200°C (392°F) and are pressed together (image **3**), forcing the material to fill the mold cavity. The molds are held closed for 60 to 90 seconds (depending on the thickness of the material) and the part is revealed when they are separated (image **4**). The excess material has flowed through designated channels between the molds to ensure that it can be easily removed in a process known as de-flashing.

PaperFoam is available in a range of colours (image **5**). Lighter colours have a more consistent visual appearance, whereas the darker colours look mottled. The pigments are the same as those used in the printing industry.

Plastic Extrusion

Polymerized thermoplastic, elastomer or bioplastic powder is extruded as rods that are then cut into granules. They are further processed by extrusion or molding into finished products. Co-extrusion is used to form products with two or more colours in a single material or to combine dissimilar materials seamlessly.

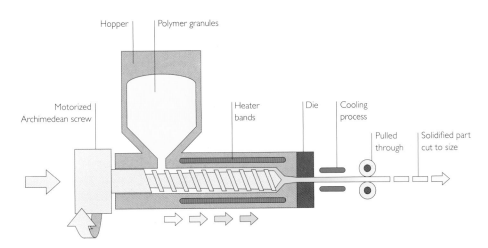

Hopper

Polymer granules

Motorized
Archimedean screw

Heater
bands

Die

Cooling
process

Pulled
through

Solidified part
cut to size

Essential Information

VISUAL QUALITY	●●●●●○○○
SPEED	●●●●●●●○
SET-UP COST	●●●○○○○○
UNIT COST	●●○○○○○○

Environmental impacts per kg

ENERGY	●●○○○○○○
RESOURCES	●●○○○○○○
POLLUTION	●○○○○○○○
WASTE	●●○○○○○○

Related processes include:
- Co-extrusion
- Extrusion

Alternative and competing processes include:
- Compression Molding
- Injection Molding

What is Plastic Extrusion?

Similar to injection molding (page 104), polymer granules are fed from the hopper into the barrel where they are simultaneously heated, mixed and moved towards the die by the rotating action of the Archimedean screw.

The melted plastic is forced through the profiled die and into a water tank to solidify the hot polymer. Film and sheet extrusions are cooled as they pass between sets of cooling rollers rather than a water tank. This helps to control the wall thickness and apply texture.

The extruded length is cut to length or rolled up, depending on the flexibility of the material and the application.

Notes on Environmental Impacts

Extrusion is a fundamental step in the process of manufacturing plastic and bioplastic. Inevitably, heat and water are consumed in this industrial process and, therefore, the material will determine the environmental impact of the finished products (see Plastics, page 20 and Bio-based Plastics, page 24).

If a single type of material, or colour, is being produced then all the waste can usually be directly recycled: it can be put back into the hopper and re-extruded. However, mixed materials cannot be recycled as readily and so are often down-cycled into dark coloured products. Composite materials, such as wood plastic composite (WPC), may be more energy efficient to produce as raw material, but recycling and disposal can be more complicated.

Colour, brightener and fluorescing pigments The range of colours achievable in plastic is almost limitless. Transparent plastics, such as acrylonitrile butadiene styrene (ABS), polystyrene (PS) and cellulose acetate (CA), colour very well.

Fluorescent pigments glow brightly because they absorb light in the ultraviolet portion of the spectrum and emit light in the visible portion. Therefore tinted materials will appear brighter than their surroundings because they emit more visible light.

Case Study

Extruding Polymer Powder into Sheet Material

Featured company Mazzucchelli
www.mazzucchelli1849.it

The polymerized powder is fed into the hopper and heated, melted and extruded as a continuous thread (images **1** and **2**). It is run straight into cold water to begin the cooling process. In line with the extrusion process, the parallel threads run through a spinning chopper that cuts them into granules (image **3**). The granules are carefully dried and packaged.

The next step is to add colour. This is achieved by re-extruding the polymer pellets, but this time with pigment added to the mix (image **4**). The granules of cellulose acetate (CA) are injection molded (page 104) into products such as lenses, toys, tool handles or hair ornaments. Alternatively, they can be extruded into sheets (image **5**) that are used for eyewear, jewelry and handbags.

1

2

3

4

5

What is Co-extrusion?

In this process two or more polymers are extruded using conventional equipment and mixed in the co-extrusion die. They are hot and plastic (softened), which means that as they are brought together the polymers combine to form a strong bond. The joint is controlled by the design of the die. The process is suitable for combining materials of different colours (see opposite) or with different properties.

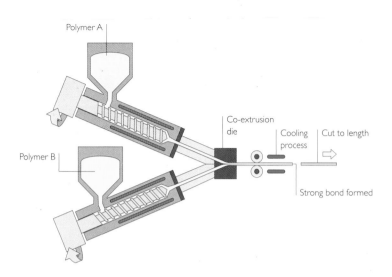

Polymer A

Co-extrusion die

Cooling process

Cut to length

Polymer B

Strong bond formed

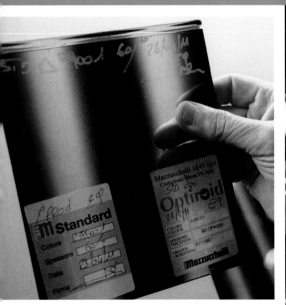

Decorative effects Mazzucchelli have devised many innovative ways to co-extrude multi-coloured sheets of cellulose acetate (CA). These materials are used to make eyewear frames, jewelry and other fashion accessories. Originally developed to mimic tortoiseshell and ivory (see forming tortoiseshell-effect with cellulose acetate, pages 32–33), CA has become a desirable material in its own right and is used to make the highest quality eyewear.

By co-extruding colours, using gradients (see far left) and even polishing away the top surface (see near left), a myriad of beautiful effects can be achieved. The colours are tailored to fit the latest trends in fashion.

1

Case Study

Co-extruding Multi-coloured Sheets of Cellulose Acetate

Featured company Mazzucchelli
www.mazzucchelli1849.it

The colours are extruded separately and brought together in the co-extrusion die (image **1**). The material is drawn through polished calendaring rolls to smooth and homogenize the hot plastic into an accurate profile (image **2**).

Each strip is cut to length and checked for visual defects (image **3**). The cross-section shows how the different colours have been combined to create a precise visual gradient on the surface (image **4**).

2

3

4

Molding Recycled Plastic

Plastic from post-consumer or industrial waste streams can be remanufactured without significant reprocessing. The materials are sorted, cleaned and flaked in preparation for molding. Alternatively, if the plastic is from a controlled source – or a closed-loop system – then it can be manufactured directly into new products.

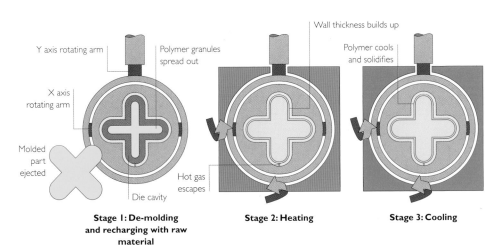

Y axis rotating arm

X axis rotating arm

Molded part ejected

Die cavity

Polymer granules spread out

Hot gas escapes

Stage 1: De-molding and recharging with raw material

Wall thickness builds up

Stage 2: Heating

Polymer cools and solidifies

Stage 3: Cooling

Essential Information

VISUAL QUALITY	●●●●○○○
SPEED	●●●●○○○
SET-UP COST	●●●●○○○
UNIT COST	●●●●○○○

Environmental impacts per kg	
ENERGY	●●○○○○○
RESOURCES	●○○○○○○
POLLUTION	●○○○○○○
WASTE	○○○○○○○

Related processes include:
• Rotation Molding
• Sheet Molding

Alternative and competing materials include:
• Glass
• Metal
• Paper and Board

What is Rotation Molding?

Rotation molding produces hollow forms with a constant wall thickness. Polymer powder is tumbled around inside the mold to produce virtually stress-free parts. Surface finish is good even though no pressure is applied.

In stage 1, a predetermined measure of polymer powder is loaded into the mold. It is closed, clamped and transferred to the heating chamber. In stage 2, it is heated to around 280°C (536°F), which is the same as for virgin polyethylene (PE), for around 30 minutes and is constantly rotated around its horizontal (x) and vertical (y) axes.

As the walls of the mold heat up the powder melts and gradually builds up an even coating on the inside surface. The thickness is controlled locally: higher temperature produces a thicker wall section. In stage 3, the mold is transferred to a cooling chamber for around 30 minutes.

Once the parts have cooled sufficiently they are removed from the molds. The whole process takes between 30 and 90 minutes, depending on wall thickness and choice of material.

Notes for Designers

QUALITY The design should accommodate the incorporation of 100% recycled materials because this will affect colour, reliability and certain mechanical properties. For example, recycled PE is more ductile at ambient temperatures, so the rotation-molded kayak (see below) requires additional structural elements, such as ribs in the hull.

TYPICAL APPLICATIONS Almost any type of product can be produced from remanufactured materials. Exceptions include applications that require materials that are free from contamination, for instance, food packaging and medical products.

COST AND SPEED Recycled plastics are usually less expensive than virgin plastics (page 20). For example, the recycled kayak is 20% less expensive for the customer than one made from virgin PE. However, demand for high quality recycled material is increasing and so in some cases the cost is rising.

MATERIALS Thermoplastics, including polypropylene (PP), PE, polycarbonate (PC), polyvinyl chloride (PVC) and polystyrene (PS).

ENVIRONMENTAL IMPACTS Recycled plastics are simply flaked and then molded. Nothing is added during molding – except that heat is required – and there is very little waste, if any. Recycling 1 ton (2,204 lbs) of plastic saves around 1.5 tons (3,307 lbs) of carbon dioxide equivalent emissions. The source of the materials is critical because inconsistent quality and any contamination will affect the properties of the finished product.

Case Study

Recycling Plastic Kayaks

Featured company Palm Equipment Europe
www.palmequipmenteurope.com

It is essential that the recycled material is high quality and of the same composition. Therefore, Palm Equipment only use waste high density polyethylene (HDPE) from their factory and products they have made which have been returned at the end of their useful life. The scrap is cut and shredded at the factory (image **1**).

The mold is prepared with release agent and graphics and, 17.5 kg (38.5 lbs) of HDPE, which has been carefully ground to the correct particle size, is evenly distributed inside (image **2**). The same weight of material is used compared to virgin PE, but the bulk density of recycled powder is significantly lower due to the reprocessing (grinding produces a 'fluffier' powder). This means that the wall thickness is slightly greater in recycled versions.

The mold is clamped shut and loaded into the heating chamber (image **3**). Due to the length of this product it is molded in a chamber that rocks back and forth while the mold rotates inside (image **4**). This in effect rotates it around each axis 360°. Once the mold is sufficiently cool the kayak is removed (image **5**) and the accessories and safety equipment are fixed in place (image **6**).

1

2

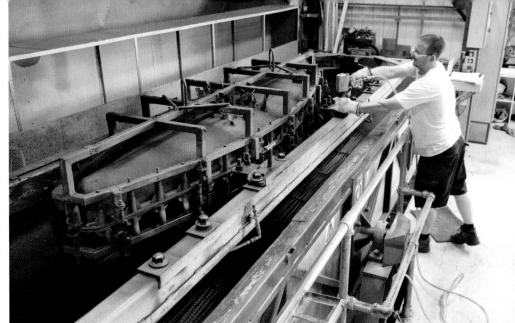

3

4

5

6

What is Recycled Plastic Sheet Molding?

This is a straightforward compression molding process (page 110). In stage 1, a pre-determined weight of material is loaded into the molds. Sheet sizes range from 1.2 x 0.8 x 0.003 m (47.2 x 31.5 x 0.1 in.) to 3 x 1.5 x 0.025 m (118 x 59 x 1 in.), weighing 3 kg to 110 kg (6.6–242.5 lbs) respectively.

In stage 2, the mold halves are pressed shut and heated to between 140°C (284°F) for polyvinyl chloride (PVC) and 180°C (356°F) for polycarbonate (PC). This causes the plastic particles, flakes or pellets to melt together. Once the plastic has cooled sufficiently the parts of the mold separate and the sheet is removed. The whole process takes between 30 minutes and four hours depending on sheet thickness.

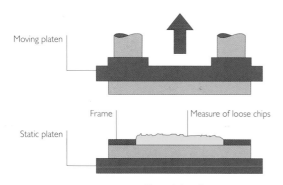

Moving platen
Frame | Measure of loose chips
Static platen

Stage 1: Loading

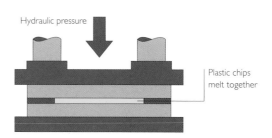

Hydraulic pressure

Plastic chips melt together

Stage 2: Sheet molding

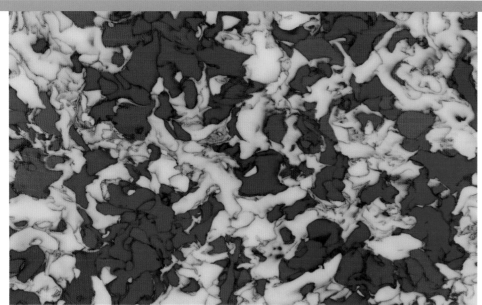

Recycled blue water pipes and yellow gas pipes
The materials do not mix completely during molding, so the sheets are colourful, random and unique. Smile Plastics produce a wide range of sheet materials from recycled plastic. The majority are PE or PS, commonly used in packaging, furniture and industrial applications. They are available in a wide range of vivid colours, which are ideal for this type of material. Other feedstock includes compact discs (PC), bank notes, wellington boots (PVC) and even scrap from their own factory.

Case Study

Molding a Sheet from Post-consumer Recycled Plastic Packaging

Featured company Smile Plastics www.smile-plastics.co.uk

Using 100% recycled materials eliminates the energy required to produce the same quantity of raw material. This process converts disposable packaging, including oil drums, into sheet materials that can be used to make new products – for instance, chairs, tables, counters and lighting.

The recycled material in this case is flaked HDPE detergent bottles (image **1**). The material, weighing 24 kg (53 lbs), is spread out in the 1 x 2 x 0.012 m (39.4 x 78.7 x 0.5 in.) mold (image **2**). The size of chip, colour and additives all affect the final appearance.

The mold is closed and loaded into the hydraulic press (image **3**) along with several other molds. After molding, the sheets are removed (images **4** and **5**) and cut to size.

Composite Laminating

Fibre reinforcement is combined with a rigid plastic matrix to form light and strong parts. The many benefits of composites are driving demand in aerospace, high performance automotive and racing boat applications. Material development aimed at reducing the environmental impact includes bio and recycled composite.

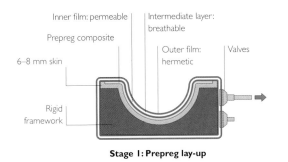

Inner film: permeable
Prepreg composite
6–8 mm skin
Rigid framework
Intermediate layer: breathable
Outer film: hermetic
Valves

Stage 1: Prepreg lay-up

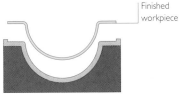

Finished workpiece

Stage 2: De-molding

Essential Information

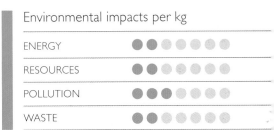

VISUAL QUALITY	●●●●●●○○
SPEED	●●●○○○○○
SET-UP COST	●●●●○○○○
UNIT COST	●●●●●●○○

Environmental impacts per kg

ENERGY	●●○○○○○○
RESOURCES	●●○○○○○○
POLLUTION	●●●○○○○○
WASTE	●●○○○○○○

Related processes include:

• Prepreg   • Wet Lay-up

Alternative and competing processes include:

• Compression Molding   • Injection Molding
• Veneer Laminating

What is Prepreg Composite Laminating?

Prepreg uses sheets of fibre reinforcement that have been pre-impregnated with plastic matrix (see Biocomposite Prepreg, page 98 and FibreCycle, page 17). The sheets are either woven or unidirectional. The matrix supports and bonds the fibres, transferring applied loads and protecting the fibres from damage.

In stage 1, the layers of prepreg are laid into the mold. The whole assembly is encapsulated within three layers of material: a permeable blue film, a breathable intermediate membrane and an outer hermetic film. This ensures that an even vacuum can be applied to the whole surface area.

The prepreg lay-up is placed into an autoclave at 4.14 bar (60 psi) and a temperature of 120°C (248°F) for two hours. In stage 2, the finished part is de-molded.

Notes for Designers

QUALITY The mechanical properties of the product are determined by the combination of materials and lay-up method. Typically, only the side in contact with the mold can be gloss. It is possible to produce parts with a gloss finish on both sides, but this adds complexity and leads to other compromises.

TYPICAL APPLICATIONS Applications are becoming more widespread and include racing cars, boat hulls, structural framework in aeroplanes and furniture.

COST AND SPEED Tooling costs and labour costs are moderate to high as moldmaking is a labour-intensive process. Cycle time varies: a small part might take an hour or so, whereas a large, complex one may take as many as 150 hours.

MATERIALS Conventional materials utilized in this process include carbon, glass and aramid fibre reinforced plastic (CFRP, GFRP and AFRP). Laminating thermosetting resins include polyester, vinylester and epoxy.

ENVIRONMENTAL IMPACTS Harmful chemicals are used in the production of CFRP, GFRP and AFRP, and it is very difficult to recycle scrap or the products at the end of their life. However, exciting recent developments have made it possible to start recycling CFRP (see FibreCycle, page 17).

Alternatively, plant fibres such as hemp, jute and flax (page 94) can be used for the fibre reinforcement and it is possible to use thermoplastics (simpler to recycle than thermoset, see Plastics Recycling, page 208), bioplastic (page 24) or recycled plastic for the resin matrix. These material developments are significantly reducing the environmental impact of composites.

Alternating weave The direction and alignment of the weave affects the mechanical performance of the part. For high performance products this is calculated using finite element analysis (FEA) software prior to manufacture. In this case, each layer of twill prepreg is alternated 45° to ensure maximum strength across the part.

1

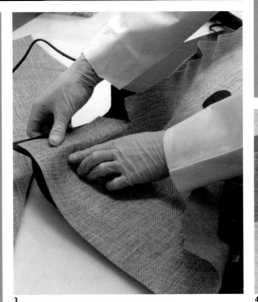

2

3

4

Case Study

Laminating with Biocomposite Prepreg

Featured company Lola Group
www.lola-group.com

These body parts for the Lola/Drayson racing Le Mans Prototype electric car (image **1**) were sponsored by the Warwick Innovative Manufacturing Research Centre (WIMRC) at Warwick Manufacturing Group. The ultra-high-performance electric vehicle, based on an existing Lola chassis, was launched in 2011.

The sheets of flax prepreg are prepared by hot-melt processing (page 99). They arrive laminated between sheets of protective release film, which are removed (image **2**). A CNC plotter is used to cut the profile directly from CAD data.

The layers of twill-woven prepreg are placed into the mold at 45° to the previous layer (see image, opposite). As each layer is added it is rubbed down to ensure the corners and finer details are reproduced precisely (images **3** and **4**).

Case Study

Vacuum Bag and Autoclave

Featured company Lola Group
www.lola-group.com

When all the layers of prepreg are in place the entire molding and tool are covered with a permeable blue film (image **1**). This is overlaid with a layer of breathable membrane and the mold is then placed inside a pale pink hermetic film (image **2**). The resulting 'sandwich' enables a vacuum to be applied to the mold: this forces the laminate onto its surface (images **3** and **4**).

The vacuumed mold is then placed into an autoclave, which cures the resin with heat and pressure (image **5**). Many molds are placed in the autoclave for each two-hour cycle.

1

2

3

4

5

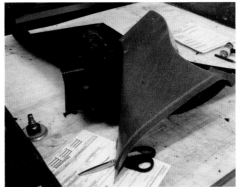

1

2

Case Study

De-mold and Finish

Featured company Lola Group
www.lola-group.com

Once cured, the part is removed from the mold (images **1** and **2**). Cutting lines are built into the mold and so are easily highlighted on the finished part with a white chinagraph pencil (image **3**). Holes are drilled for fixings. The profile is then cut out and finished (image **4**).

It is possible to reproduce complex shapes and small radii with prepreg (image **5**). The weave will determine the design opportunities. Plain weave is very stable, but difficult to wrap into complex profiles, whereas twill and satin weaves are more flexible and can reproduce deep profiles.

3

4

5

Basket Weaving

The techniques used in basket weaving are ancient and depend on local materials and traditions. All types of natural, pliable and fibrous materials are used, including willow, cane, leaf and bark. Handcrafted, locally sourced and renewable materials have no negative impacts on the environment.

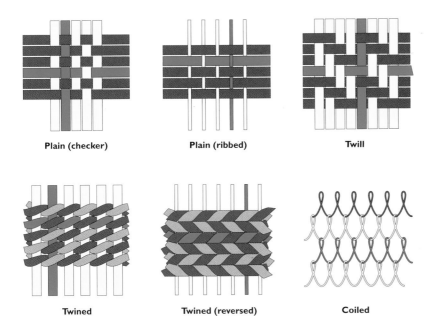

Plain (checker) **Plain (ribbed)** **Twill**

Twined **Twined (reversed)** **Coiled**

Essential Information

VISUAL QUALITY	●●●●●○○
SPEED	●●●●○○○
SET-UP COST	●●●●●○○
UNIT COST	●●●●●○○

Environmental impacts per kg

ENERGY	●●●●●●●
RESOURCES	●●●●●●●
POLLUTION	●●●●●●○
WASTE	●●●●●●○

Alternative and competing processes include:
- Injection Molding
- Rotation Molding
- Thermoforming

What is Basket Weaving?

A plain weave can be made from palm, birch bark, leaf, reed, or similar. The warp (vertical strands) and weft (horizontal strands) are the same width and cross at right angles, alternately passing over and under one another to produce a checkered pattern. Using rigid warp ribs and flexible weft strands produces the familiar willow basket texture. Groups of wefts may be bunched together (see opposite).

Twill weaving is also a 0 and 90 degrees technique. Each warp is passed over two wefts and under two wefts and vice versa. The resulting diagonal pattern is known as twilled.

Twining uses rigid warp strands. The wefts are grouped together in twos or threes and wound around each other as they are alternately woven over and under the warps. Alternatively, the twist in the wefts is reversed in each row, producing a more densely packed weave.

Coiled baskets are made by looping string or rope together. Traditionally, flexible materials such as cotton, willow, raffia and straw are used.

QUALITY Baskets are lightweight and durable. The visual quality is largely dependent on the materials, which in turn determine the techniques used. Natural materials will result in variation.

TYPICAL APPLICATIONS Baskets are used for storage, fishing and packaging. Other applications include sunshades, furniture (mainly upholstery and screens), hats (such as the famous Panama) and bags.

COST AND SPEED There are no tooling costs, but hand tools are used. Cycle time is moderate to long and labour costs are moderate to high depending on the size and design.

MATERIALS Suitable natural fibrous materials include grass, leaves, bark, rattan, willow, reed and bamboo. The typical materials depend on location. For example, willow is common in the UK, bamboo in China and birch bark in subarctic countries such as Finland.

ENVIRONMENTAL IMPACTS Plant materials are harvested from local and renewable sources and minimal transportation is required. Weaving is carried out by hand so there is no need for energy consuming machinery. Natural materials are biodegradable and do not transmit any harmful elements into the environment.

Willow rods and finished baskets Willow was once very common in the UK. It is managed and harvested in spring or winter when the rods have reached 1.2 m (4 ft) or more in length. After cutting, the rods are graded by length. Brown willows are rods dried and used with their bark intact. Buff willow is boiled for several hours and the bark is removed. White willow is peeled without boiling. The rods are soaked in water for several days in preparation for weaving and then stored in a cool and damp environment for a day or two to 'mellow'.

1

Case Study

Weaving a Willow Basket

Featured company English Willow Basketworks
www.robandjuliekingbasketmakers.co.uk

Even though there is a global market
for basket weaving materials, it is best
to acquire local and renewably sourced
material (image **1**). This determines the
type of material and thus the quality and
volume of products that can be made.

Traditionally, baskets are made to fulfil
a specific need and the design has evolved
as a consequence. First of all a sturdy round
base is formed by weaving thin flexible rods
around an arrangement of thicker bottom
sticks (image **2**). The upright 'stakes' are
inserted alongside the bottom sticks and
bent upwards, supported by a woven ring
(image **3**). More willow weavers are woven
tightly around the stakes in a process
known as 'upsetting'. The sides of the basket
are then woven. The top is finished with
a border of stakes, which are folded down
and woven into the round structure (image
4). This is known as a 'common' border.
Finally, a roped handle is formed and woven
into the border (image **5**). It is a robust
construction made up of a thick core
wrapped with thinner, flexible rods.

2

3

4

5

Steam Bending

Combined with joinery, steam bending is used to shape curved wood for furniture, boats and buildings. The advantage of bentwood over machining is that the grain runs continuously along its length, utilizing the inherent strength of wood and minimizing waste.

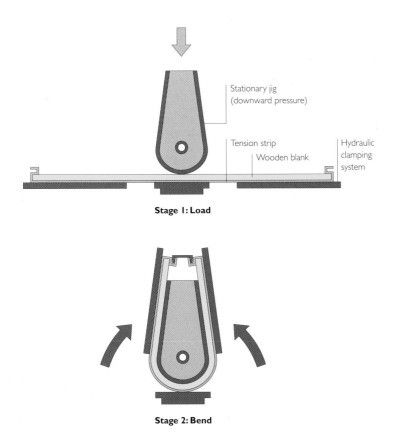

Stage 1: Load

Stationary jig
(downward pressure)

Tension strip

Wooden blank

Hydraulic
clamping
system

Stage 2: Bend

Essential Information

VISUAL QUALITY	●●●●●●○
SPEED	●●●●○○○
SET-UP COST	●●○○○○○
UNIT COST	●●●●●○○

Environmental impacts per kg

ENERGY	●●○○○○○
RESOURCES	●●○○○○○
POLLUTION	○○○○○○○
WASTE	○○○○○○○

Alternative and competing processes include:
- CNC Machining
- Wood Laminating

What is Steam Bending?

Bentwood is either formed by hand or with a hydraulic or rotary press. Hand forming can be used to make a range of different profiles, but the bend radius and diameter of the wood being bent are limited compared to power-assisted processes. Forming by hand may also reduce the energy required (see also Basket Weaving, page 132).

All of the processes work on the same principle: the wooden pole is softened by thermo-mechanical steam treatment. In stage 1, the wood is clamped in position onto a jig and in stage 2 it is formed around the jig.

The moisture content will affect the length of time required for steam treatment. 'Wet' or 'green' wood, which has not been kiln dried – so eliminating the associated energy – requires less steam treatment, but will take longer to dry.

Notes for Designers

QUALITY This process utilizes the inherent strengths of wood because the grain is formed into the direction of the bend. The length of the grain also affects the strength of the wood. Processes that reduce grain length, such as machining, reduce tensile and compressive strength. Wood is a naturally variable material and no two pieces will be alike.

TYPICAL APPLICATIONS Furniture, boats, timber frame buildings and a range of musical instruments use bentwood.

COST AND SPEED The jigs are usually made from timber and are not expensive. The cycle time for steam bending is quite slow: soaking (24 hours), steaming (1–3 hours) and final drying at 75°C (167°F) in an oven (24–48 hours). Labour costs are moderate to high due to the level of experience required.

MATERIALS Beech and ash are common in furniture making; oak is common in construction; elm, ash and willow are traditionally used in boatbuilding; and maple is used for musical instruments. Other suitable timbers include birch, hickory, larch, iroko and poplar. Rattan (climbing palm) is not a timber, but it can be shaped by steam bending.

ENVIRONMENTAL IMPACTS Steam bending timber from a renewable source is a low impact process. A relatively small amount of energy is required to produce the steam and run the machinery. The jigs and machinery are typically long lasting and used to produce tens of thousands of parts. There is little waste, which can be used as biofuel.

Case Study

Steam Bending the Loveseat

Featured company Ercol www.ercol.com

Lucian Ercolani designed the Loveseat in 1956. The seat is solid elm and the bentwood backrest, spindles and legs are beech. It is available in natural or painted black (image **1**) (see also, Water-based Coating, page 158).

Ash for the backrest is air-dried until the moisture content is around 25% and so it remains 'green' (not kiln dried). It is roughly cut to length, soaked in water and steamed at 104°C (219°F) in a pressure chamber at 0.6 bars (8.7 psi) for up to 3 hours (image **2**). This makes the wood adequately pliable by softening the lignin, which bonds the cellulose together.

The wooden strips are loaded in batches of four into a mechanical open-bending press (images **3** and **4**). Force is gradually increased and the wood is bent around the stationary jig (image **5**). A metal strip is used to maintain the bend and the parts are removed from the jig inside the tensioned frame (image **6**). They are left to dry and 'set' for 24 to 48 hours. Afterwards, they are removed, profiled and assembled, using a range of joinery techniques (page 142), into the Loveseat.

2

3

4

5

6

Case Study

Manually Bending the Evergreen Chair

Featured company Ercol www.ercol.com

The Evergreen Chairs each have a
bentwood beech backrest (image **1**).
The shape indicates that this design is
a descendant of the traditional English
Windsor chair of the Chiltern woodlands.
It has been in production since the 1950s.

Steam bending relies on a tensioning
strip, which is held on the outside edge
of the wooden blank (image **2**). Wood
will compress when the lignin becomes
plastic, but it will tear very quickly if it is
stretched more than 1% of its length. The
tensioning strip ensures that the bend is
formed by compression.

Together with the tensioning strip,
the wood is manually bent around the
jig (image **3**). Manual bending is used
because the wood is bent in more than
one direction. The carpenters work in
unison to maintain an even force along
the length of the wood and twist it as they
go to maintain the tensioning strip along
the outside of the bend profiles. This
helps to minimize spring-back and
maximize strength.

Once formed, the bentwood is left
in the jig to set (image **4**). The part is
removed (image **5**), profiled by hand with
a spoke shave (image **6**) and sanded to a
smooth finish. It is assembled (see Joinery,
page 142) and is ready to be lacquered
(image **7**).

1

2

3

4

5

6

7

Wood Joinery

Furniture constructed from renewably sourced timber using joinery and water-based adhesive is high quality, long lasting and repairable. Wood can be left untreated or it can be protected with a water-based coating. The small amount of waste is used as biofuel.

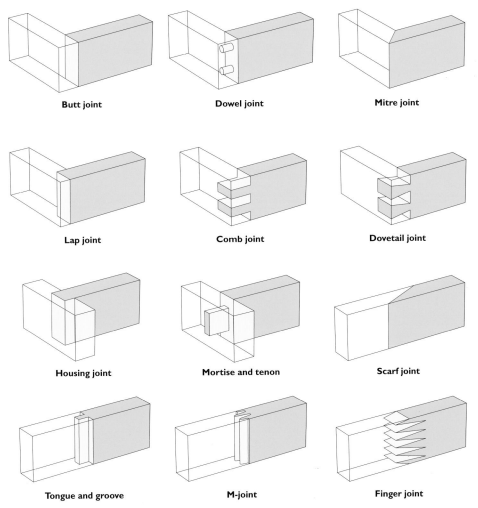

Butt joint

Dowel joint

Mitre joint

Lap joint

Comb joint

Dovetail joint

Housing joint

Mortise and tenon

Scarf joint

Tongue and groove

M-joint

Finger joint

Essential Information

VISUAL QUALITY	●●●●●○○
SPEED	●●●●○○○
SET-UP COST	●●●○○○○
UNIT COST	●●●●●○○

Environmental impacts per kg

ENERGY	●●○○○○○
RESOURCES	●○○○○○○
POLLUTION	●●○○○○○
WASTE	●●●○○○○

Related Processes include:

- Butt Joint
- Dovetail Joint
- Finger Joint
- Lap Joint
- Mitre Joint
- Scarf Joint
- Comb Joint
- Dowel Joint
- Housing Joint
- M-joint
- Mortise and Tenon
- Tongue and Goove Joint

Alternative and competing processes include:

- Timber Frame Construction
- Veneer Laminating

What is Wood Joinery?

Joinery is an essential part of furniture making and house building. There is a standard set of joints and many variations. The most common types include butt, lap, mitre, housing, mortise and tenon (page 146), M-joint, scarf, tongue and groove, comb (page 147), finger (page 148) and dovetail (page 144).

There are many variations: for example, tongue and groove or mortise and tenon can utilize a loose tongue or tenon (page 150). In other words, it is a separate piece of material. In contrast, a tenon that passes right through can be wedged for added strength (page 149).

There are many types of adhesive: PVA is water-based and non-toxic, while excess glue can be cleaned from the joint with a wet cloth. The alternatives include urea formaldehyde (UF), two-part epoxies and polyurethane resin (PUR).

Notes for Designers

QUALITY Products will have unique characteristics associated with the qualities of wood. The quality of a joint is very much dependent on skill. Joints can be extremely precise, especially when using CNC machining.

TYPICAL APPLICATIONS Joinery is used in woodworking industries, including furniture and cabinet making, construction, interiors, packaging, boat building and patternmaking.

COST AND SPEED Some applications require jigs, but these are typically low cost and long lasting. Cycle time is totally dependent on the complexity of the job. Labour costs tend to be quite high, but CNC processes reduce these costs for high volumes.

MATERIALS The most suitable wood for joinery is solid timber (page 56) such as oak, ash, beech, pine and birch.

ENVIRONMENTAL IMPACTS Joinery typically requires the removal of material and the addition of adhesive. However, there is very little waste and it can be incinerated as biofuel (at Ercol the waste is incinerated and the energy is used to heat the factory and provide hot water) or used for other processes such as in the production of bioplastic (page 24). Modern CNC systems have very sophisticated dust extraction. Specifying local materials from renewable sources helps to reduce environmental impacts further. Energy and resources are required to maintain the machinery and provide heating and lighting.

Case Study

Dovetail and Mortise and Tenon Joints in a Windsor Sideboard

Featured company Ercol www.ercol.com

The Ercol Windsor Sideboard (image **1**) is made from solid elm. It includes dovetail joints in the cabinet and drawers, and mortise and tenon for the uprights (see also, mortise and tenon joints, page 146). Dovetail joints are similar to finger joints (page 148), but are cut with angled sides, which increase the strength of the joint in certain directions. They are especially useful for drawers, which are repeatedly pulled and pushed from the front. In this case, they are cut on a CNC router (image **2**) and include a shallow rebate, which will house the adjoining part (image **3**).

The structure is assembled and the uprights are secured with mortise and tenon joints (images **4** and **5**). It is smoothed over with a belt sander (image **6**), the drawers are assembled (image **7**) and the finished piece is ready for coating with water-based lacquer (page 158).

1

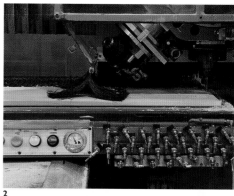
2

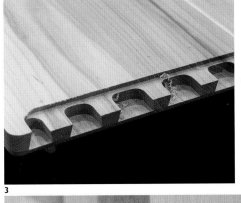

3

4

5

6

7

Case Study

Mortise and Tenon Joints

Featured company Ercol www.ercol.com

Mortise and tenon joints are used to join perpendicular lengths of wood. There are many different types including haunch, shoulder, blind, through, loose (see using jigs and loose tenon joints in a Katakana occasional chair, page 150) and pegged.

The leg is the tenon (image **1**) and the mortise is the hole (image **2**). The grain runs along the length of the wood (tenon), which is perpendicular to the length of timber that has the mortise cut into it (image **3**). Strength is greatest in the direction of the grain.

They can also be cut on round profiles. For this sofa arm (image **4**) tenons are cut into the ends and mortises across the grain (image **5**). The parts are assembled (image **6**) and the profiled tenon shoulders fit snuggly against the round part (image **7**).

1

2

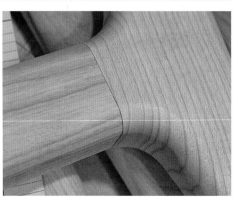

3

4

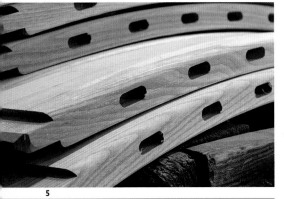

5

6

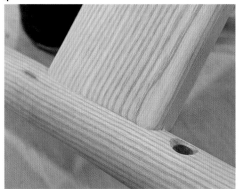

7

Case Study

Comb Joint in a Drawer

Featured company Ercol www.ercol.com

Comb joints (also called finger joints) are extremely strong. In fact, they are one of the only joints that cannot be 'knocked' apart once the glue has started hardening: this is because there is such a large surface area. The joints are made by a series of spaced cutters on a spindle molder and by a spinning cutter that profiles lengths or ends of wood (image **1**).

This is a common joint for boxes and drawers. The sides are assembled (image **2**) and a belt sander is used to finish both sides simultaneously (image **3**). The finished joint shows end grain on both faces (image **4**).

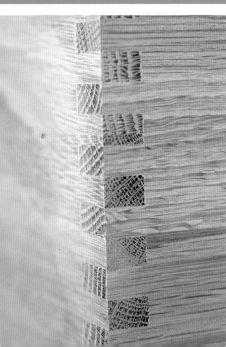

Case Study

Finger Joint in a Chair Seat

Featured company Ercol www.ercol.com

The finger joint is machine made and designed to integrate lengths of timber into a continuous profile. It maximizes the gluing area and joint strength (images **1** and **2**). Once assembled and glued, the part is profiled by CNC machining. The layers of the joint are revealed in the front face where it has been cut at an angle (image **3**). This makes up part of the seat in the High Back Easy Chair (see Steam Bending, page 136).

1

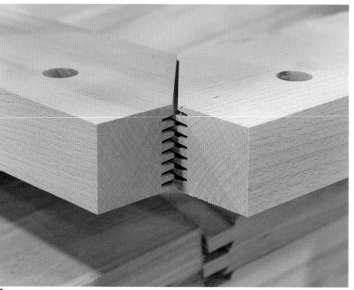

2

3

1

Case Study

Wedged Joints in an Arm Rest

Featured company Ercol www.ercol.com

Mortise and tenon or dowel joints that penetrate right through can be further strengthened by driving a wedge into the tenon in the direction of the grain. The joint consists of a mortise (cut right through), a tenon (with a slot) and a wedge (image **1**).

Glue is applied, the tenon is inserted into the mortise and the wedge is driven into the joint (image **2**). This forces the tenon to spread outwards and fill the joint mortise completely.

When the glue is sufficiently dry it is cut off and sanded flat (image **3**). The wedge and end grain of the tenon are visible on the surface of the finished joint (image **4**).

2

3

4

Case Study

Using Jigs and Loose Tenon Joints in a Katakana Occasional Chair

Featured company Dare Studio
www.darestudio.co.uk

Sean Dare designed the Katakana Occasional Chair for Dare Studio in 2010. It is manufactured by Edwin Lock Furniture in solid oak or walnut (image **1**). The joinery is unique and complex: nothing is perpendicular. The skilled carpenter uses a portable router, called a Domino, to cut the mortises. This is a unique joining system developed by Festool. It uses pre-fabricated beech tenons that have a large gluing area and cannot be rotated (like a dowel). It produces a very strong joint. Cutting two mortises creates less waste than a conventional mortise and tenon.

Each piece is cut and assembled using jigs to ensure accuracy when cutting and gluing (image **2**). The router produces a neat, repeatable mortise and the loose tenon is glued in place (images **3**, **4** and **5**). It is assembled and, once the glue has dried, the profile is made (image **6**).

The back is assembled in the same way using an array of jigs, clamps and straps (images **7** and **8**). After joining and coating, the chair is upholstered (image **9**).

1

3

2

4

5

6

7

8

9

Upholstery

This is the process of making and bringing together the hard and soft parts of a piece of furniture into the finished article. The majority of the environmental impact is are therefore related to the materials, which include a timber frame, steel springs, webbing, padding, cushioning and a cover.

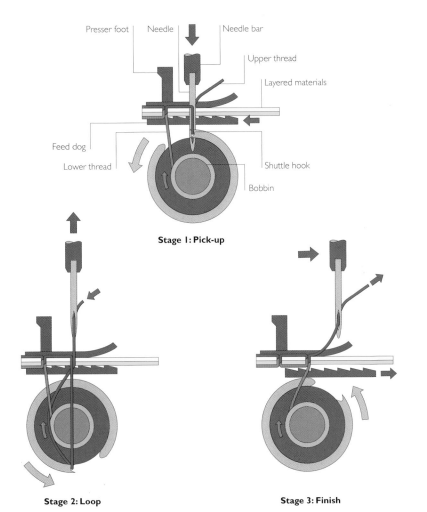

Presser foot Needle Needle bar

Upper thread

Layered materials

Feed dog

Lower thread

Shuttle hook

Bobbin

Stage 1: Pick-up

Stage 2: Loop

Stage 3: Finish

Essential Information

VISUAL QUALITY	●●●●●●○
SPEED	●●●○○○○
SET-UP COST	●●○○○○○
UNIT COST	●●●●●●○

Environmental impacts per kg

ENERGY	●●○○○○○
RESOURCES	●●○○○○○
POLLUTION	●●○○○○○
WASTE	●●●○○○○

Alternative and competing processes include:

- Foam Molding
- Injection Molding
- Rotation Molding

What is Machine Lockstitching?

Lockstitching is a mechanized process. The needle and shuttle hook are synchronized by a series of gears and shafts, which are powered by an electric motor. In stage 1, the upper thread is carried through the textile by the needle and the lower thread is wound on a bobbin. The needle pierces the layers of material and stops momentarily. In stage 2, a spinning shuttle hook picks up the upper thread. The shuttle hook loops behind the lower thread, which is held under tension on the bobbin. In stage 3, as the shuttle continues to rotate, tension is applied to the upper thread, which pulls it tight, forming the next stitch. Meanwhile, the feed dog progresses forward, catches the fabric and pulls it into place for the next drop of the needle. The fabric is supported between the presser foot and feed dog. Industrial sewing machines can repeat this sequence over 5,000 times a minute.

QUALITY The selected materials for the frame, springs, webbing, padding and cover will affect the overall appearance and durability. Upholstery is a complex process and no two pieces of handmade furniture are exactly the same, so the final quality is largely dependent on the skill and experience of the upholsterer.

TYPICAL APPLICATIONS Furniture and interiors such as cars and boats.

COST AND SPEED Jigs may be required. Overall cycle time is reasonably long due to the number – and complexity – of the operations. Labour costs are relatively high.

MATERIALS Any fabric can be used for upholstery. The location of applications, such as home, office or automotive, determines the most suitable types. Fabrics with a high resistance to wear include wool, polyamide (PA), nylon, polyester, thermoplastic polyurethane (TPU), polyvinyl chloride (PVC) and polypropylene (PP). Other suitable materials include leather, flock, raffia, mohair, cotton and canvas.

ENVIRONMENTAL IMPACTS Upholstery is the culmination of many different processes and, in consequence, a typical sofa will include different materials that have varying environmental implications. Ensuring that each material is from a renewable and local source will ensure minimal environmental impact. Durability is determined by the least strong part in the construction, whether it is the frame, padding or cover.

Much more waste is produced when upholstering with leather, which is partly why it is more expensive. On fabric, the net shapes can be nested very efficiently, producing only 5% waste, whereas leather may have imperfections that cause up to 20% waste.

Oscar sofa Matthew Hilton designed the Oscar sofa in 2010. It is built to last and is reasonably lightweight. The combination of a European-sourced hardwood frame, jute webbing, hessian straps, animal hair, natural fibres and wool cover make this a low impact product to manufacture.

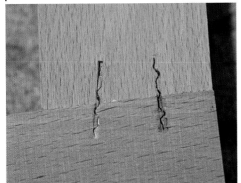

Case Study

Producing the Hardwood Frame for the Oscar Sofa

Featured companies Coakley & Cox
www.coakleyandcox.co.uk and
SCP www.scp.co.uk

The frame and internal woodwork is made from a combination of plywood (see page 62) and sawn beech timber. The sheets of birch plywood are used in the arms and cut out around a profile (image **1**). A variety of joinery techniques (page 142) are used to assemble the solid wood frame. The glued butt joints are reinforced with dowels and crimped metal plates (images **2** and **3**). The metal plate ensures the joint remains tight while the glue hardens.

The back legs are stained with walnut-coloured stain (image **4**) and the frame is ready to be upholstered (image **5**) (page 156).

1

2

3

4

5

Case Study

Upholstering the Oscar Sofa

Featured companies Coakley & Cox
www.coakleyandcox.co.uk and
SCP www.scp.co.uk

The base of the frame, where the seat
will be, is criss-crossed with elasticated
webbing (image **1**) and the back is covered
with steel 'zig zag' springs. The webbing
layers of hessian and needled wool padding
(page 84) are stapled to the timber frame.
Alternatives to wool include calico
(plain woven cotton) and polyethylene
terephthalate (PET) textile, which is known
under the trade name Dacron®. Where
required, a wool fire-barrier padding is
also stapled onto the timber frame. This
is covered over the seat area with the
finished cover which is sewn to black
bottoming cotton cloth. Upholstery is a
highly skilled process: the craftsman marks
and cuts the padding and cover to fit each
part individually (image **2**).

The arms have jute webbing (page 95)
applied and are then covered with cocoa-
lock (latex-covered coconut fibre, see
Rubber, page 36) and calico to produce
sturdy arm rests with a padded outer layer
(images **3** and **4**).

The wool cover is marked up using
stencils and is then cut out (image **5**).
Each of the panels is stitched inside out
(image **6**), so that when it is reversed on
the sofa the stitching and excess material
are concealed inside (image **7**).

The back has a line of sewn-in pulls
(images **8** and **9**) where the wool is pulled
tight against the padding. This gives the
appearance of a buttoned back without
the actual buttons.

1

2

3

4

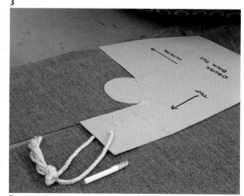

5

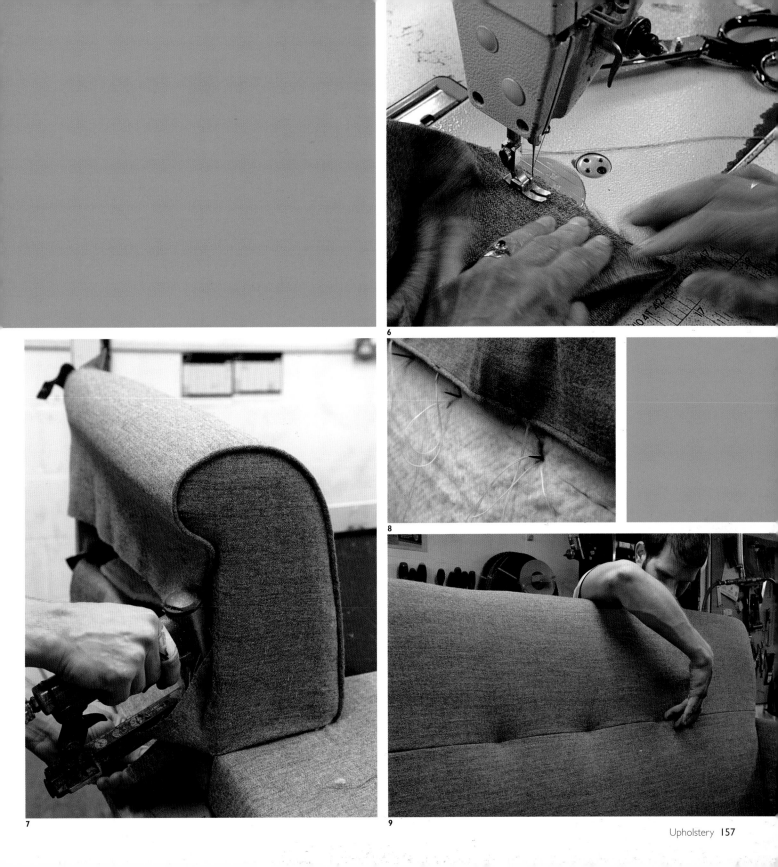

6

7

8

9

Water-based Coating

Water-based products are applied by spray, dip or flow coating. Also referred to as waterborne, they are mostly latex or acrylic polymer emulsion dispersed in water. Compared to solvent-based products, they are durable, have good visual quality, are cost effective, non-toxic and can reduce harmful emissions by 95%.

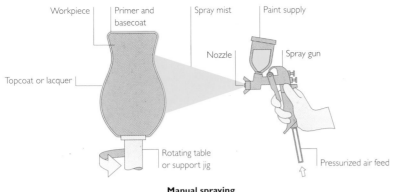

Manual spraying

Workpiece | Primer and basecoat | Spray mist | Paint supply

Topcoat or lacquer

Nozzle | Spray gun

Rotating table or support jig

Pressurized air feed

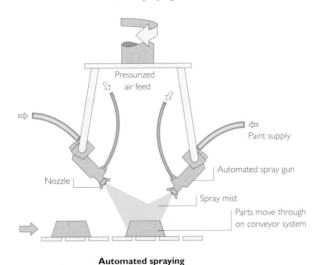

Automated spraying

Pressurized air feed

Nozzle

Paint supply

Automated spray gun

Spray mist

Parts move through on conveyor system

Essential Information

VISUAL QUALITY	●●●●●●○○
SPEED	●●●●●○○○
SET-UP COST	●●○○○○○○
UNIT COST	●●●○○○○○

Environmental impacts per kg

ENERGY	●○○○○○○○
RESOURCES	●●○○○○○○
POLLUTION	●○○○○○○○
WASTE	●●○○○○○○

Related processes include:
• Dip Coating
• Spray Coating

Alternative and competing processes include:
• Powder Coating
• Solvent-based Coating

What is Spray Coating?

Spray guns use a jet of compressed air to atomize the paint into a fine mist. The atomized paint is blown out of the nozzle in an elliptical shape. The coating is applied onto the surface in an overlapping pattern. The speed of the conveyor, or rotating jig, is optimized with the speed of painting to maximize efficiency.

Spray coating is typically a manual process that is automated for mass production. Manual coating is a highly skilled process and is more versatile for coating complex and large parts.

Automated systems are rapid and production is continuous. Either the products move through on a conveyor belt and pass underneath moving spray guns or the products are stacked into a rotating jig and coated by static spray guns.

Notes for Designers

QUALITY Finish can be very high quality and is largely dependent on the surface quality before coating and the skill of the operator. A high quality painted surface is nearly always made up of more than one layer. The level of sheen on the coating is categorized as matt (also known as eggshell), semi-gloss, satin (also known as silk) and gloss.

TYPICAL APPLICATIONS Water-based coatings have been used for some time to protect and finish automotive parts, furniture and toys.

COST AND SPEED Jigs may be required to support parts. Cycle time is good, but depends on size, complexity and finish. Labour costs are high for manual processes.

MATERIALS Many types of wood, metal and plastic can be coated with water-based products. There are many different types of paint and they have varying levels of environmental impact. Some surfaces require an intermediate coating, which is compatible with both the workpiece and the topcoat.

ENVIRONMENTAL IMPACTS Adoption of water-based coating systems has been encouraged – or enforced in some industries – by legislation. Traditional solvent-based paint systems have a significant impact on the environment, including volatile organic compound (VOC) emissions during application and toxic additives that are harmful in use (such as on toys and in terms of indoor air quality). However, there are many different types so care should be taken to assess the full list of ingredients and make sure the coating will perform well in the environment and be less harmful than solvent-based alternatives.

Case Study

Spray Painting Ercol Nest of Tables

Featured company Ercol www.ercol.com

1

Lucian Ercolani, the founder of Ercol, designed the Nest of Tables in 1956. They are made from solid timber – with elm tops and beech legs – and today are manufactured using CNC machining and wood joinery (page 142).

Ercol uses only water-based finishes. The underside is coated first (image **1**) and then the outside surfaces (images **2** and **3**). After each coat the acrylic-based paint is dried in a tunnel oven (image **4**). Drying temperature varies according to the seasons – from 20°C (68°F) in the summer to 35°C (95°F) in the winter – and takes around seven minutes. Accelerating the drying process improves efficiency and reduces the risk of dust or other surface contamination.

Water-based paints are made up of pigment, binder and additives, which are dispersed or dissolved in water. During application the water evaporates, causing the paint to dry and the pigment and binder to bond to the surface. The high water content causes the surface of the wood to swell slightly which raises the grain. It has to be rubbed down by hand in between coats using an abrasive pad (image **5**). In this case two coats are required.

The coating is not intended to cover up the wood completely: the grain and joinery are visible through the finished paint (image **6**).

2

3

4

5

6

Case Study

Coating a Quaker Chair with Tinted Lacquer

Featured company Ercol www.ercol.com

The solid ash seat, back and legs of the Quaker Chair are shaped and assembled in the factory. An advantage of water-based coating is that it can be carried out in the same space as cutting and joining – this is because there are no unpleasant fumes and these paints do not present a fire risk.

Spray coating is a line-of-sight process, so the chair is placed on a rotating table, which allows the operator to have access to all sides and angles (image **1**).

The water-based stain is wiped off the surface of the wood with a rag and the wood is prepared for lacquering (image **2**). As with spray painting colour (page 160), the lacquer is acrylic-based. However, it is clear, or only tinted with pigment, so that the natural colour of the wood is visible through the coating.

Once the first coat has dried sufficiently, the surface is rubbed down with abrasive paper (image **3**). This levels the grain, which has risen due to water absorption during coating.

The second and final coat is applied (image **4**). The darker areas around the joints and edges are created by applying a darker colour stain over the base colour before lacquering. The chairs are passed through the tunnel oven to dry the coating (image **5**). The surface is lightly rubbed down (image **6**) and waxed by hand to produce a glossy and hard-wearing finish. The tonal variation is clearly visible in the finished chair (image **7**).

1

2

3

4

5

6

7

What is Dip Coating?

Dipping into a tank of liquid coating can be a manual or automated process. It is a rapid process used to coat parts with simple geometries – i.e., without hollows or cavities.

In operation, the part is submerged in the liquid coating, removed and allowed to drain. The thickness of the coating depends on the viscosity and density of the liquid and the speed of dipping. The operator does not need to be as highly skilled as for spray coating (page 162).

Dip coating with solvent-based products generates higher quantities of VOC emissions compared to spray coating and presents a fire hazard due to the large area of liquid exposed to the atmosphere. Water-based systems do not emit VOC or present a fire hazard.

Topcoats are not applied by dipping if the quality of the finish is critical. This is because the end result is not as good as spray coating.

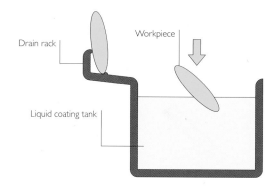

Drain rack

Workpiece

Liquid coating tank

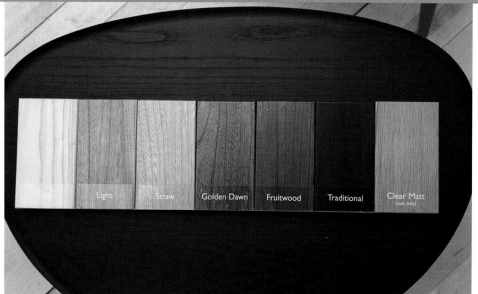

Clear Light Straw Golden Dawn Fruitwood Traditional Clear Matt (oak only)

Lacquer colour range There are many types, colours and shades of lacquer that can be applied, ranging from clear to dark and matt to gloss. It is used to protect the surface from everyday use, improve resistance to ultraviolet light (UV), emphasize the wood grain and natural patterns, tailor the colour and control the level of sheen. The concentration of pigment and dye will affect the opacity of the coating.

1

Dip Coating a Butterfly Chair

Featured company Ercol www.ercol.com

Solid elm is laminated into a curved profile for the seat and back of the chair (image **1**). Dip coating is a rapid and efficient method for applying the water-based stain to these simple, open geometries.

The parts are individually dipped (image **2**) and dried in racks to allow excess stain to run back into the tank. They are then wiped by hand (image **3**). The stained parts are stacked (image **4**) and dried in a tunnel oven. They are assembled with the beech legs and spray coated with two coats of clear lacquer (image **5**). Launched in 1958, the Butterfly Chair was designed by Lucian Ercolani.

2

3

4

5

Electropolishing

A cost-effective alternative to chrome plating stainless steel, electropolishing removes surface undulation to produce a bright lustre and a durable finish. The entire process takes place in a bath of solution, which means that small, complex, large and tubular parts are equally straightforward to polish.

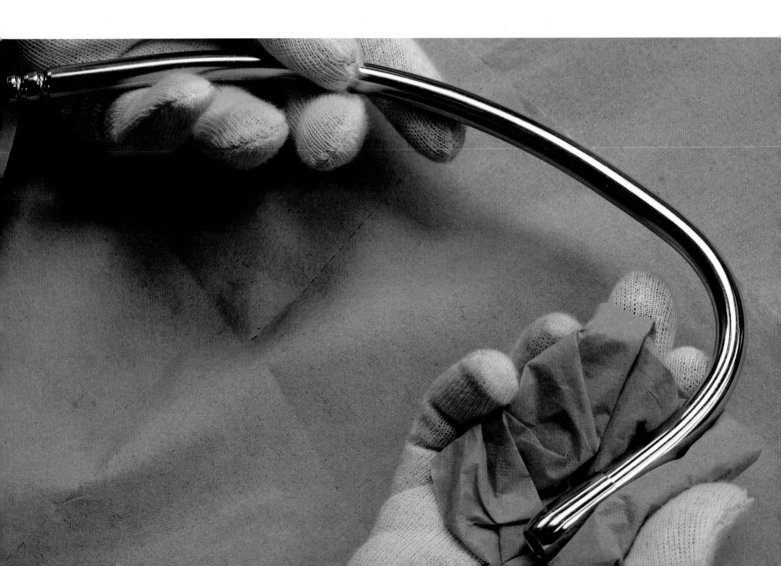

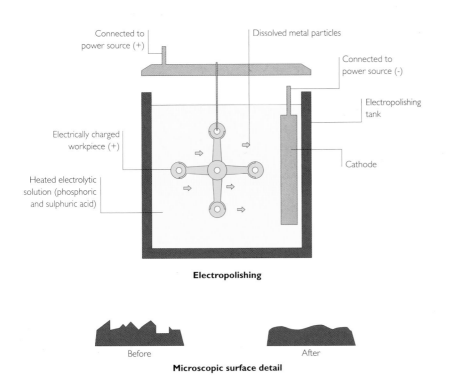

Electropolishing

Before | After

Microscopic surface detail

Connected to power source (+)

Dissolved metal particles

Connected to power source (-)

Electropolishing tank

Electrically charged workpiece (+)

Cathode

Heated electrolytic solution (phosphoric and sulphuric acid)

Essential Information

VISUAL QUALITY	●●●●●●○○
SPEED	●●●●●○○○
SET-UP COST	●○○○○○○○
UNIT COST	●●●○○○○○

Environmental impacts per kg

ENERGY	●●●●○○○○
RESOURCES	●●○○○○○○
POLLUTION	●○○○○○○○
WASTE	●○○○○○○○

Alternative and competing processes include:
- Mechanical Polishing
- Metal Plating

What is Electropolishing?

The process takes place in a bath of electropolishing solution (phosphoric and sulphuric acid). The bath is maintained at between 50°C and 90°C (122–194°F), depending on the rate of reaction: the warmer the solution, the more rapid the reaction. The workpiece is suspended on an electrically charged jig and becomes the anode (+). The cathode (-) is made from the same material and placed in the electropolishing solution.

When an electric current is passed between the cathode and the workpiece, the electropolishing solution dissolves metal particles from the surface of the workpiece. The surface detail illustrates how surface dissolution takes place more rapidly on the peaks because that is where the power density is greatest. Low points are dissolved more slowly and thus the surface of the material is gradually made smoother.

Notes for Designers

QUALITY Material removal is typically in the range of 5 to 10 microns (0.0002–0.0004 in), although it is possible to remove in excess of 50 microns (0.002 in). The final quality is largely dependent on the original surface finish and the electropolishing time. The finish is clean, hygienic and more resistant to corrosion.

TYPICAL APPLICATIONS Products include architectural metalwork, industrial applications, furniture, food and pharmaceutical applications.

COST AND SPEED Set-up costs are limited to jigs. Cycle time is good and labour costs are low. This process is 50% to 75% less expensive than metal plating.

MATERIALS It is mainly used to finish stainless steel, but can be used on all metals.

ENVIRONMENTAL IMPACTS The environmental benefits are threefold: it can replace chrome plating (which uses restricted chemicals with high risk to operator health), the surface durability of metal is improved and it is a subtractive process, so no other materials (which could delaminate or wear away over time) are added.

Although the chemical solution must be periodically replenished, approximately 25% can be reused each year, the chemicals tend to be far less hazardous to the operator and the resultant residue is more easily treated compared to other metal finishing processes.

Aesthetic and functional surface The process dissolves iron more readily than other metallic elements and this phenomenon means that electropolished stainless steels have a chromium-rich layer on the surface. This layer protects the steel from corrosion because it reacts with oxygen to form chromium oxide, which passivates the surface and makes it less reactive to atmospheric elements. As well as protecting the steel, the chromium-rich layer can be so bright that it gives the illusion of chrome plating.

Jigs Parts are suspended in the electropolishing baths mounted onto jigs. The design of the jig is critical to ensure even surface removal and to allow liquid to drain away quickly, reducing contamination between the baths.

1

2

3

Case Study

Electropolishing Metalwork

Featured company Firma Chrome Ltd
www.firma-chrome.co.uk

The stainless steel rings are formed and assembled without surface finishing. One of the benefits of electropolishing is that the liquid solution is able to get into all the parts of such a complex assembly (image **1**).

The rings are mounted onto racks on a rotating frame (image **2**). The parts are dipped in the baths in sequence: polishing, neutralizing and rinsing. Electropolishing takes 10 minutes or so when the parts are electrically charged. The green acidic solution drains off the parts as they are removed from the tank (image **3**). They are washed for a final time to remove any remaining contamination (image **4**).

4

Risography

This high speed and low cost stencil duplicator printing process is commonly called risography, or Riso, after the Japanese manufacturer of the same name. Riso printers use soy inks, are energy efficient, operate at room temperature and do not create harmful by-products.

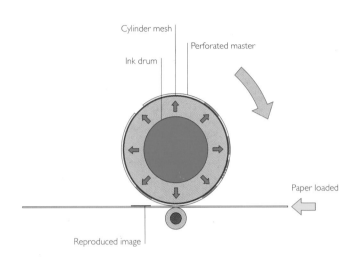

Cylinder mesh

Perforated master

Ink drum

Paper loaded

Reproduced image

What is Risography?

Like screen printing (page 174), this is a stencil printing process. The master is produced from a thin paper-plastic laminate. It is created from a digital file or by scanning an original. The image areas are burnt out of the plastic layer and the master is wrapped around the drum.

Ink containers are loaded into the cylinder around which the master is wrapped. As the cylinder rotates at high speed, the ink is pressed through the cylinder mesh screen by an internal squeegee roller that sandwiches the paper with another roller outside the drum.

The paper is registered to the location of the master and passes underneath. Ink is applied to the surface. Modern presses can reproduce up to 150 pages per minute (ppm). Each colour requires its own master. Presses are either one or two colour. If more colours are required then the ink drums are changed and the paper is passed through the machine a second time.

QUALITY Registration is not precise (see below) and stencil duplicator printing has a distinctive appearance as a result of the perforated paper master. The inks are bright and include fluorescents.

TYPICAL APPLICATIONS It is used to produce low cost flyers, posters, stationery, books, fanzines, art prints and magazines.

COST AND SPEED Cycle time is up to 150 pages per minute. The master costs are minimal. It is generally an inexpensive process, but is less cost effective than offset lithography (page 181) for high volumes.

MATERIALS Paper.

ENVIRONMENTAL IMPACTS Riso printers use 95% less energy than laser printers because they do not require heat to fuse toner onto the page. They do not produce air pollutants such as toner particles and silica dust, which reduce air quality. Chemical cleaning is not required because the master is disposable.

Soy ink is less expensive and less energy intensive to produce than petroleum-derived inks and it contains fewer volatile organic compounds. A small amount of ink is needed and it is easily removed in the de-inking process used in paper recycling. However, the source is critical because it can affect food production and increase prices locally.

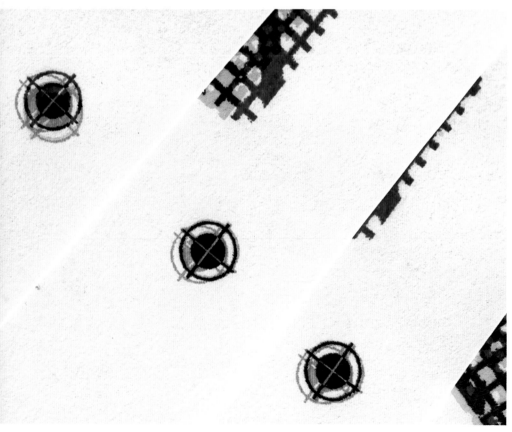

Registration marks Registration is not precise in multi-colour printing, but inaccuracy can be minimized by a skilled operator. Heavy outlines help to reduce the visual impact of misalignment and this misalignment can be used to artistic advantage, differentiating this process from high volume automated production such as offset lithography.

Colours can be overlaid and are not disturbed by secondary printing using another process such as digital printing.

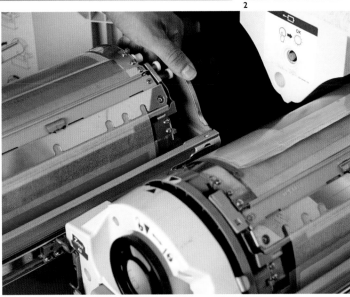

1

Case Study

Printing a Wolff Olins Poster

Featured company Ditto Press www.dittopress.co.uk

Jack Gilbey designed this poster for an exhibition of works by Geetika Alok, Charlotte Coulais, Jack Gilbey and Hiromi Suzuki at Wolff Olins (image **1**).

Ink drums are dedicated to a colour (image **2**). The ink is loaded inside and the master is wrapped around the cylinder screen automatically. After each job the master is discarded. It uses minimal material, but is difficult to recycle because it is laminated paper and plastic.

The ink drums are interchangeable (image **3**), so they can be used to apply any number of colours. This poster is made up of four colours: after the first two colours have been printed in this two-colour press, the ink drums are changed and the second two are applied to produce the final print (image **4**).

2

3   4

Water-based Printing

Using water-based inks reduces the environmental impact of screen printing. They do not contain harmful chemicals, solvents or plastics and can be washed away with water. They can be printed onto paper, metal and textiles, and in the latter case replace plastisol ink, which contains polyvinyl chloride (PVC).

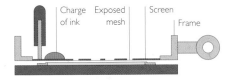

Stage 1: Load

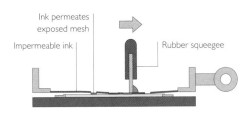

Stage 2: Screen print

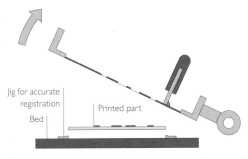

Stage 3: Unload

Essential Information

VISUAL QUALITY	●	●	●	●	●	●	○
SPEED	●	●	●	●	○	○	○
SET-UP COST	●	○	○	○	○	○	○
UNIT COST	●	●	●	●	○	○	○

Environmental impacts per kg

ENERGY	●	○	○	○	○	○	○
RESOURCES	●	●	○	○	○	○	○
POLLUTION	●	●	○	○	○	○	○
WASTE	●	○	○	○	○	○	○

Related processes include:

- Screen Making
- Screen Printing Textiles

Alternative and competing processes include:

- Digital Printing
- Transfer Printing

What is Water-based Screen Printing?

This is a wet printing process and is the same for all types of ink: a charge of ink is deposited onto the screen and a rubber squeegee is used to spread the ink evenly across the screen. Those areas protected by the impermeable film (stencil) are not printed.

The screens are made up of a frame over which a light mesh is stretched. In stage 1, the mesh is set just above the surface of the material and registered. In stage 2, the squeegee is drawn across the screen, forcing it onto the surface of the material. The ink then goes through the unmasked areas. The screen is under tension and so it pulls itself away from the printed material. This avoids the ink smudging and bleeding. In stage 3, the finished print is removed.

QUALITY   Screen printing produces graphics with clean edges. The definition of detail and thickness of printed ink is determined by the size of mesh, i.e., the gauge, used in the screen. Heavier gauges will deposit more ink, but have lower resolution of detail.

TYPICAL APPLICATIONS   Screen printing is used to reproduce artwork, exhibition graphics and stationery and for textile products such as bags, clothes and fabrics for interior applications.

COST AND SPEED   Set-up costs are low, but depend on the number of colours because an individual screen is required for each colour. Water-based screen printing is suitable for low volumes and mass production. Labour costs are moderate to high for manual processes.

MATERIALS   Almost any material can be screen printed, including paper, plastic, rubber, metal, ceramic and glass. However, water-based inks cannot be used on all materials, so compatibility must be checked.

ENVIRONMENTAL IMPACTS   Water-based inks contain less harmful ingredients than petroleum-based equivalents. After printing, the ink is washed from the screen with water and the solids are separated before it enters the sewage system. By contrast, waste petroleum-based inks have to be disposed under hazardous waste regulations.

Detail and half tone   Gradients are produced by reducing the area of ink to dots, known as half tone. As the concentration of dots for each colour is reduced, the visible colour changes. This technique is used in all printing. The dots will be visible close up.

Mesh size will affect the quality of the half tone. It is determined by the number of threads (38–380 imperial and 15–150 metric) and thread diameter: 31, 34 or 40 (small, heavy or medium). Fine details require high thread counts and small diameter thread. However, using tighter meshes reduces the amount of ink applied and can affect the opacity of the print.

This graphic was designed by Kiosk for Nottdance 07 Festival by Dance 4 and is printed on organic cotton.

1

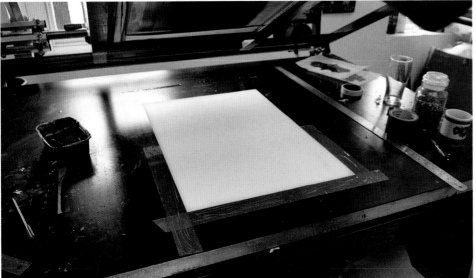

2

Case Study

Screen Printing a Poster

Featured company I Dress Myself
www.idressmyself.co.uk

The screen is registered with the master (image **1**) on the screen-printing bed. It is covered with ghost images leftover from previous print runs. The screens are recycled by dissolving the impermeable film away from the mesh and recoating it with emulsion.

The poster is loaded onto the bed and registered (image **2**). All printing at I Dress Myself is done by hand. The screen is lowered over the poster and ink is drawn across the mesh with a squeegee (image **3**). The colour of the ink is similar to the colour of the emulsion mask on the screen.

The posters are carefully set aside to dry in racks (image **4**). Water-based inks take several hours to dry unless they contain co-solvents which reduce drying time.

3

4

Colour In the past, the use of water-based inks has been limited to printing on light-coloured textiles. Recent developments include more opaque inks, thicker consistency, intense colours and fluorescents suitable for printing on dark colours. This has resulted in designs such as this one by Alun Edwards for Multiple.

Handle This bag by Timo Juntto for Fuga has a large area of print. Unlike plastisol inks, water-based inks do not affect the handle (feel) of the fabric – and lighter colours affect the handle least of all.

Case Study

Two-colour Printing a T-shirt

Featured company I Dress Myself
www.idressmyself.co.uk

Designed by Elliot Baddeley and Dryden Williams for Valley Clothing, the inks are mixed according to a master reference (image **1**). A white T-shirt is stretched onto the screen-printing bed on the carousel (image **2**). This is rotated after each stage of printing.

Pink is applied, followed by blue (images **3** and **4**) and the print is checked against the master (image **5**). The mottled effect is produced using half tone.

The printed T-shirts are passed through a tunnel heater at 270°C (518°F) for one to two minutes. This evaporates all of the water and fully cures the ink (image **6**).

Care must be taken to ensure water-based inks do not dry in the screens: they would clog the mesh and ruin the screen. To ensure this does not happen, the screens are washed after each print run (image **7**). This also applies if a print job lasts more than one day: the screens must be washed out at the end of each day. At I Dress Myself the water is passed through a pebble and limestone filter before entering the sewer system.

1

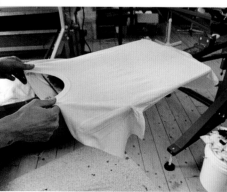

2

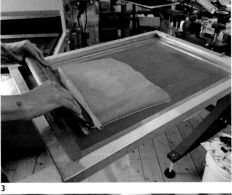

3

4

5

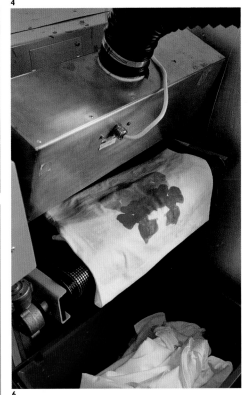

6

7

Waterless Printing

The waterless technique is a high quality printing process very similar to conventional offset lithography. However, the environmental impact of this process is significantly less: water, volatile organic compounds (VOC), chemicals and waste are significantly reduced, while printing speed is increased.

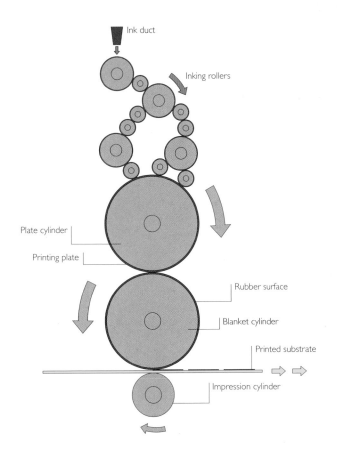

Ink duct

Inking rollers

Plate cylinder

Printing plate

Rubber surface

Blanket cylinder

Printed substrate

Impression cylinder

Essential Information

VISUAL QUALITY	●●●●●●●
SPEED	●●●●●●○
SET-UP COST	●●●●●○○
UNIT COST	●●○○○○○

Environmental impacts per kg

ENERGY	●●○○○○○
RESOURCES	●●○○○○○
POLLUTION	●○○○○○○
WASTE	●●○○○○○

Related processes include:
- Sheet-fed
- Web-fed

Alternative and competing processes include:
- Flexography
- Risography
- Screen Printing

What is Waterless Offset Lithographic Printing?

Conventional offset lithography relies on the principle that oil and water do not mix. The non-image areas on the printing plate absorb water, whereas the image areas repel water. In waterless printing, the use of water is replaced by a silicone coating on the printing plate. The image areas of the plate are etched away to reveal the ink-receptive plastic layer beneath.

The ink is transferred to the rubber surface on the blanket cylinder, which is pressed against the paper as it rotates, creating a sharp and well-defined print.

A disadvantage of removing water is that the plates and cylinders heat up. Cooling systems are required to maintain the temperature between 21 and 29.4°C (70 and 85°F).

Notes for Designers

QUALITY Waterless printing produces very high quality prints with consistent colour, very good colour saturation (ink density is 20% higher than for conventional offset lithography) and low dot gain (see below).

TYPICAL APPLICATIONS These include packaging, labels, books, magazines, newspapers and similar products.

COST AND SPEED Set-up costs are high – a little more than conventional offset lithography, but unit costs are equivalent – making this process less practical for short production runs. Cycle time is rapid: web-fed presses can print hundreds of metres per minute.

MATERIALS The choice of paper and board is greater than for conventional offset lithography and includes coated and uncoated stock. Other suitable materials include metal and plastic.

ENVIRONMENTAL IMPACTS Park Lane Press saves an estimated 70,000 litres (18,500 gallons) of filtered water, 8,000 litres (2,100 gallons) of VOCs, 30–40% paper and significant amounts of electricity and ink per year compared to conventional offset lithography (based on running two B2 size presses three shifts a day).

Eliminating the fount solution (water and other chemicals used in the dampening system of conventional offset lithography) means there is no need to use isopropanol (or a substitute) and other chemicals that are absorbed into paper during printing. Soy ink is less expensive and less energy intensive to produce than petroleum-derived inks and it contains fewer VOCs.

Print quality Ink is printed as dots. As the concentration of dots for each colour is reduced, the visible colour changes. This is known as half tone, which is measured as lines per inch (lpi). Dot gain is the result of ink spreading on the surface of the printed material. It is inevitable, but is significantly less in waterless printing because the ink is more viscous and the 'intaglio' etched surface of the printing plate creates pockets (dark areas on the green print plate) that hold the ink in place. Details and colour can therefore be printed more accurately than with conventional offset lithography.

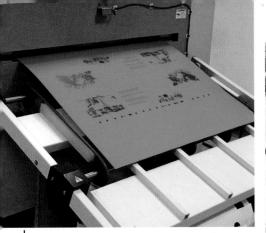

1

2

3

Case Study

Printing a Brochure

Featured company Park Lane Press
www.parklanepress.co.uk

The plate for each colour is produced
directly from computer data in a process
known as computer to plate (CTP). The
green silicone coating is etched away in
the image areas (image **1**).

An operator keys the level of ink to
be applied to each part of the ink roller
(image **2**) and the plate is loaded into
the press (image **3**). As with conventional
offset lithography, waterless is a four-colour
process (image **4**). The process colours are
cyan, magenta, yellow and ketone (black),
which are known collectively as CMYK.
For specific colours and effects, such
as fluorescent and metallic, spot colours
are used.

The quality of the prints is checked for
registration (alignment), colour and printing
defects such as rub-off and smudging
(image **5**).

4

5

Lifecycle

3

Recover, Refurbish, Reuse

End-of-life products can be recovered, refurbished, rebuilt and reused to reduce cost, consumption of resources and production of emissions. Electronics and vehicles contain many valuable components and materials, which can be dismantled and recovered or separated to improve the recovery rates in recycling.

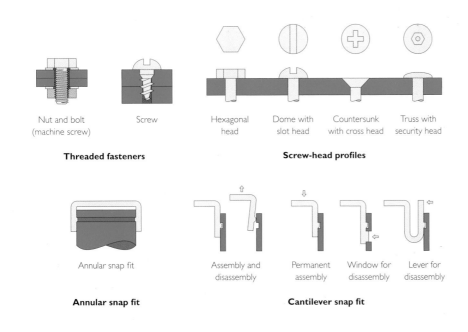

Nut and bolt (machine screw)　　Screw

Threaded fasteners

Hexagonal head　　Dome with slot head　　Countersunk with cross head　　Truss with security head

Screw-head profiles

Annular snap fit

Annular snap fit

Assembly and disassembly　　Permanent assembly　　Window for disassembly　　Lever for disassembly

Cantilever snap fit

Essential Information

TRANSPORTATION	●●○○○○○
CLEANING	●○○○○○○
REPROSSESSING	●●●●●●○

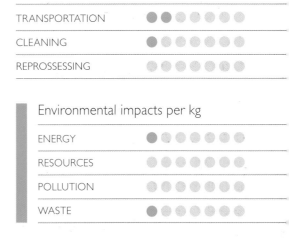

Environmental impacts per kg

ENERGY	●○○○○○○
RESOURCES	●●●●●●○
POLLUTION	○○○○○○○
WASTE	●○○○○○○

Related systems include:
- Recovery
- Reuse
- Refurbish

Alternative and competing systems include:
- Mixed Recycling
- Plastic Recycling

What is Design for Disassembly?

Products made up of more than one material, or component, are designed for disassembly (DfD) to ensure that useable and valuable parts can be removed for reuse or recycling. It is also important to be able to remove harmful materials to avoid their ending up in landfill.

Mechanical fasteners enable DfD, whereas laminating, adhesive bonding and other permanent fixing methods make disassembly impractical or impossible. Threaded fasteners are a versatile means of assembly: the main types are bolts (small diameter bolts are also referred to as machine screws) and screws. Bolts have a cylindrical shaft and helix thread and are held in place by threading into a nut or threaded hole (known as tapped). There are many hundreds of types of screws, including wood, self-tapping, thread rolling, drywall, dowel and so on. The type of screw depends on the materials and application.

Mechanical fixings are designed into parts wherever possible to avoid adding unnecessary materials and operations. For example, injection molded (page 104) and blow molded parts can be designed with integrated snap fits.

DESIGN Products built with durable materials and designed to allow for maintenance or upgrading are more likely to be refurbished and reused. Eventually products will need to be disassembled and recycled and therefore they should be designed so that the materials can be separated (especially hazardous ones such as batteries) for recovery. Using the same fixings throughout, or as few different types as possible, helps to improve recovery rates. For example, Dell computers use only one or two types of fasteners. A dismantler can take these products apart more quickly than products made using many different types. Snap fits are preferable to screws.

APPLICATIONS The principal industrial reuse schemes include the WEEE (Waste Electrical and Electronic Equipment) and the ELV (End of Life Vehicles) directives. The success of these is mainly due to the impact of legislation on the producers, distributors and recyclers. Returnable and reusable packaging is another good demonstration of widespread and continued reuse (page 194). In some cases, technology limits what can be reused – for instance, currently there is no certified solution for data wiping solid state hard drives (although this is under development), so they have to be destroyed.

COST Designing with consideration for end-of-life reduces the total environmental impact and can help to reduce cost. Regulations are put in place to encourage the adoption of processes and technologies that reduce emissions, waste, consumption of resources and production of harmful waste. This change can increase cost in the short term, especially if new equipment is needed, and noncompliance can result in hefty fines. Ultimately, reducing waste and improving efficiency saves money.

Case Study

Refurbishing Computer Equipment

Featured company Sims Lifecycle Services
www.simsmm.com

Technology products, such as computers, servers, scanners, printers, copiers and telephones, can be refurbished. It is estimated that reusing a computer saves around 1.8 tons (4,000 lbs) of resources.

Stringent data wiping standards are in place to ensure all data is securely destroyed. Devices arrive on palettes (image **1**) and are marked with a barcode, which is scanned into the Asset Register program to identify the products that need secure data wiping. Sensitive data can be wiped before the devices leave the building in which they were used.

Banks of laptops are processed using Blancco® Data Cleaner (image **2**). Each computer is thoroughly tested and if a software data wipe does not work then the hard drive will be destroyed. Once processed, the laptops are thoroughly cleaned inside and out (images **3** and **4**). They are usually redeployed within an organization, sold to recoup some of their initial cost or donated.

1

2

3

4

Case Study

Computer Equipment Recovery and Recycling

Featured company Sims Lifecycle Services
www.simsmm.com

Equipment that is beyond economic repair is dismantled to recover the metals and plastics for recycling. First the mechanical fixings that secure the housing are removed (images **1** and **2**). Modern technology products are being designed so that they can be efficiently disassembled – for example, by labelling the mechanical fixings and indicating the order in which they should be removed (image **3**).

This is partly due to legislation introduced to reduce the amount of electronic equipment being produced and to encourage recovery, reuse and recycling. For example, the WEEE directive was introduced in the UK in January 2007. In addition, the EU batteries directive aims to reduce the impact on the environment of the manufacture, distribution, use, disposal and recovery of batteries (considered hazardous waste). Batteries are now removed to be recycled separately (image **4**). The Restriction of the Use of Certain Hazardous Substances in Electrical and Electronic Equipment (RoHS) directive will make products less hazardous for recycling.

Metals and plastics are valuable for recycling (page 208). Metals with high resale value, such as gold and palladium, are used in processors and printed circuit boards (PCBs) in laptops, desktop computers and other electronic equipment. Once separated, they can be recovered more effectively (images **5** and **6**). In this way, material recovery rates can be as high as 95%.

Even though the computers are not fit for repair, the parts may be reusable. Memory, hard drives and processors are reconditioned for resale (image **7**).

1

2

3

4

5

6

7

Case Study

Refurbishing Wooden Furniture

Featured company Zaxos Stathopoulos (ZS Studio)
www.zoundsystemsstudio.com

Normally pieces of wooden furniture that
are damaged beyond repair are disposed
of. It is possible to recycle the wood into
biofuel or animal bedding, for example,
or skilled craftsmen can convert battered
furniture into a unique piece (image **1**).

The surface is cracked and gouged (image
2). First the structure of the chest is made
secure (image **3**). Woodworm-eaten and
rotten parts are treated or removed. Then,
rather than filling the surface and applying
a colour topcoat, a range of polyester-
based fillers is mixed to correspond to the
layers of colour already in the chest – to
accentuate the repairs (images **4**, **5** and **6**).

The finished piece is bright and colourful
(image **7**). The unique patterns created
represent the years of use, damage and
decay combined with the craftsmanship
used to make the repairs.

2

3

1

4

5

6

7

Returnable Packaging

Returnable packaging is a reuse system that is well established in some countries. For example, UK milk bottles are returned up to 30 times. Collecting or returning, cleaning and sterilizing consume significantly less energy than manufacturing new products or packaging.

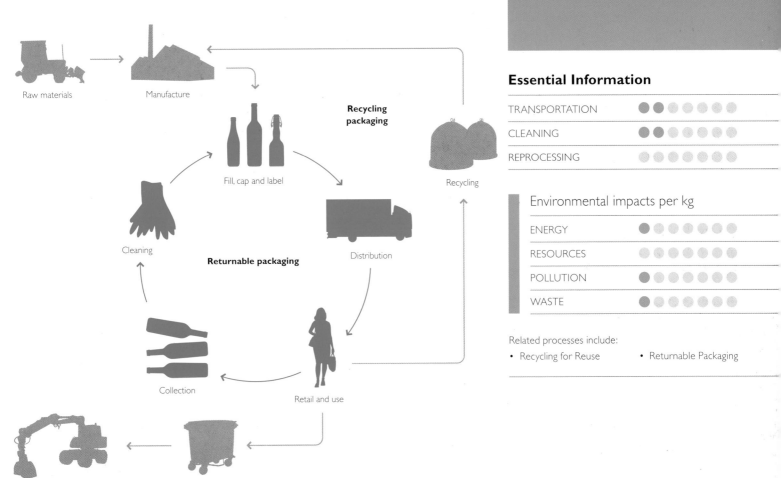

Raw materials

Manufacture

Recycling packaging

Fill, cap and label

Recycling

Cleaning

Returnable packaging

Distribution

Collection

Retail and use

Landfill

Disposal

Essential Information

TRANSPORTATION	●●○○○○○
CLEANING	●●●○○○○
REPROCESSING	○○○○○○○

Environmental impacts per kg

ENERGY	●○○○○○○
RESOURCES	○○○○○○○
POLLUTION	●○○○○○○
WASTE	●○○○○○○

Related processes include:
- Recycling for Reuse
- Returnable Packaging

What is a Returnable Glass Packaging System?

The glass industry is continually reducing emissions and improving efficiency. Recycling is a fundamental part of glass production and helps to reduce its environmental impact (page 216). However, reuse eliminates the melting and forming of glass and so saves a very significant amount of energy and emissions.

Glass packaging is distributed to the factory where it is filled, capped and labelled. In a closed-loop system the product is sold to the customer – perhaps requiring distribution – and after use the empty packaging is returned to the factory. If the bottles are chipped or damaged they can be recycled.

Glass is a durable and high quality material. Once returned to the factory, the containers are cleaned and prepared for filling, capping and labelling. It is estimated that reusing glass containers saves 95% of the emissions associated with glass manufacture.

Notes for Designers

DESIGN Returnable packaging must be optimized for cleaning, filling and storage. It should be lightweight (returnable packaging is often heavier and more robust) to reduce the environmental impact of many journeys. A minimal design will be applicable to more applications. In the case of recycling for reuse (page 194), the product should be designed for disassembly (DfD) to ensure cost effectiveness.

APPLICATIONS Successful and large-scale returnable packaging systems include the Finnish drink bottle and British milk bottle. Glass milk bottles are reused 10 to 30 times, depending on location. Returnable packaging is not permitted in all industries due to potential harmful contamination.

According to a lifecycle analysis commissioned by the British Glass Manufacturers Association, each ton of glass reused would save 843 kg (1,858 lbs) of carbon dioxide-equivalent emissions, which is almost three times as much as recycling saves. It also saves 1.17 tons (2,579 lbs) of raw materials.

Returnable packaging is often heavier and more robust, so it is essential that there are incentives to encourage customers to reuse it many times.

COST Returnable packaging will normally be more expensive than disposable packaging. This should be offset by the number of times the packaging is reused, supported by incentives for returning the bottles after use.

Case Study

Returning Glass Bottles

Featured company Whin Hill Cider
www.whinhillcider.co.uk

Whin Hill Cider take their carbon footprint seriously. The orchard is located near the bottling plant and is rich in flora and insects (image **1**). They recycle, recover heat, use lightweight bottles and, most importantly, they have a closed-loop returnable system for the bottles. This saves their business around 6,000 bottles a year, which is equivalent to 2,400 kg (5,291 lb) of glass.

The returned bottles are inspected to make sure there are no defects, the labels are removed and they are thoroughly cleaned (image **2**). They are filled with apple juice or cider (image **3**) and capped. Pasteurizing is carried out at 70°C (158°F) for 20 minutes (image **4**). This extends the shelf life of the contents and reduces waste.

Not all the bottles are labelled (image **5**) – they offer a discount for unlabelled sales. The finished goods are sampled (image **6**).

I

2

3

4

5

6

Mixed Recycling

Recycling is complex because products often contain a mix of ingredients. Our awareness of the value of materials and the finite nature of the planet's resources, combined with legislation, means that designers should consider how their products can be recycled and how the materials are extracted.

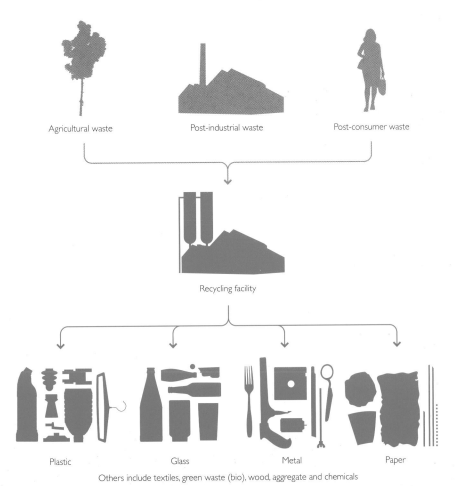

Agricultural waste

Post-industrial waste

Post-consumer waste

Recycling facility

Plastic   Glass   Metal   Paper

Others include textiles, green waste (bio), wood, aggregate and chemicals

Essential Information

TRANSPORTATION	●●●●○○○○
CLEANING	●●●●○○○○
REPROCESSING	●●○○○○○○

Environmental impacts per kg

ENERGY	●●○○○○○○
RESOURCES	●○○○○○○○
POLLUTION	●○○○○○○○
WASTE	●○○○○○○○

Alternative and competing systems include:
- Recovery and Reuse
- Returnable Packaging

What is Mixed Waste Recycling?

Materials at the end of their useful life are recycled. For instance, packaging may be recycled days after it has been manufactured, or cars and furniture several years after manufacture.

The aim of mixed waste recycling is to sort complex waste streams into different materials so they can be reprocessed. Plastic (page 208) includes waste from post-consumer packaging, waste electrical and electronic equipment (WEEE) – including consumer electronics and white goods (domestic appliances) – industrial waste and end-of-life vehicles (ELV). Metal (see also Steel, page 40, Aluminium, page 44 and Copper, page 48) includes ELV parts, industrial waste, circuitry and WEEE parts. Glass (page 216) comes from packaging, buildings, WEEE screens and ELV, whereas paper (page 212) comes from post-consumer waste, packaging and office waste. Once separated (see depollution, page 202, shredding, page 202 and separating mixed materials, page 206), the materials can be recycled into new products.

Notes for Designers

DESIGN Recyclers have developed processes capable of dealing with highly complex waste streams. However, it is still challenging to separate laminated, adhesive-bonded or otherwise permanently joined materials. Products made of a single material will be more efficient to recycle. If a mix of materials is required then products should be designed for disassembly (DfD).

APPLICATIONS All types of products can be recycled. The type of material (its suitability for recycling) and ease with which the materials can be separated determines the likelihood of its being recycled into new products. There are many examples of effective recycling systems. For example, an aluminium drink can is converted into a new can just 60 days after being placed in the recycling bin and without any loss of quality. Recycling aluminium only uses 5% of the energy required to produce virgin material. However, not all materials are recycled to make new products of the same quality. For example, recycled steel from ELV is likely to have a small amount of copper contamination. The recovered steel is down-cycled to make re-bar (reinforcement bars for concrete construction) rather than a new car or an application of equal quality. Sophisticated systems are used to separate materials and produce the highest quality recycled material. Even so, it is very difficult to keep contamination out without producing some waste. A balance is found between the quality required and waste produced (high purity inevitably means more waste).

COST In most cases recycled materials are less expensive than virgin materials because fewer resources are required to produce them. The specific cost will depend on whether the recycled material is high purity or a blend of materials.

Case Study

Preparing Mixed Waste for Recycling

Featured company Sims Metal Management
www.simsmm.com

Materials to be recycled come from a variety of sources, including domestic, post-consumer and industrial waste streams. Metals are separated into three types: heavy, sheet metal and light iron.

   Heavy, such as this steel train carriage (image **1**), is cut into smaller pieces using an oxyacetylene torch or a large guillotine. This helps with logistics and ensures that it fits in the recycling furnace (see Steel, page 40). Sheet metal (including packaging) may be separated out using grabs (image **2**). Some typical mixed waste sources include ELV (image **3**) and WEEE (image **4**). The ELV have already been through a process of depollution and crushing (page 202). WEEE scrap includes consumer electronics, white goods and other electronics that cannot be reused (page 199).

I

2

3

4

What is Metal Shredding?

Mixed materials (mostly metallic) are shredded in a fragmentizer. This process mechanically sorts mixed materials, whether they come from ELV, bikes or trolleys, for example. From the shredder three main groups of materials are recovered: ferrous material, copper armatures and a non-ferrous material (mostly non-metallic). The material goes onto the dense media plant for further separation (page 206).

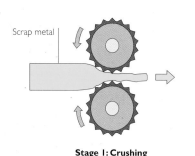

Scrap metal

Stage 1: Crushing

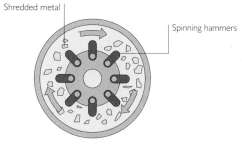

Shredded metal

Spinning hammers

Stage 2: Shredding

(page 206)

Case Study

Shredding Scrap Metal

Featured company Sims Metal Management
www.simsmm.com

Before the materials can be reclaimed, ELV are dismantled and large metal structures are broken into smaller parts (image **1**). Parts that can be reused, have particular value for recycling (such as catalytic converters) or are hazardous (such as mercury switches, airbags and seatbelt pre-tensioners) are removed from ELV. Also the battery, wheels, glass and other large components (such as plastic bumpers and seat foam) are removed to improve the recovery rates.

Then the car is depolluted. An operator drains away the fluids, including break fluid, oil, coolant and fuel (images **2** and **3**). The liquids are collected in separate tanks and are either recycled by specialists or have to be disposed of.

Depolluted cars are crushed (image **4**) and transferred to the shredder. The shredder, which is regularly opened for servicing (image **5**), consists of large hammers attached to a rotating shaft. Hammers removed after service show the wear and tear (image **6**). The metals are broken down into fragments of a suitable size for further processing (image **7**).

1

2

3

4

5

6

7

Case Study

Sorting and Shredding Waste Electronics

Featured company Sims Recycling Solutions
www.simsrecycling.com

Waste electrical and electronic equipment (WEEE) includes all sorts of materials, such as precious metals in the circuitry, which need to be separated and reclaimed. A mixture of domestic, industrial and office appliances are collected for recycling (image **1**). Most products arrive intact (image **2**) and are split into high grade and low grade. High grade, such as computers, are dismantled by hand to improve recovery rates of materials. Some parts contain valuable materials, such as the memory (image **3**), while others are considered hazardous – for instance, the batteries and liquid crystal displays (LCD) – and so have to be removed.

The remaining parts of the product are separated into the materials groups such as metals and plastics (images **4** and **5**). Prior to mechanical processing, the WEEE parts are hand sorted to remove valuable or hazardous items from the mix of materials (image **6**). For example, batteries and copper wire are removed for quality control. The plastics are passed through an initial shredding process, which breaks them down to 100 mm (3.9 in.) or so (image **7**). These are cleaned and refined into reusable plastics materials.

1

2

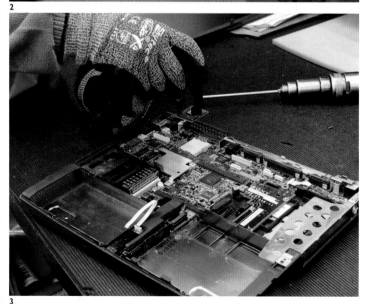

3

4

5

6

7

What is Separating Mixed Waste?

The specific characteristics of each material, such as density and iron content, are used to separate the different materials. First the overband magnet separator draws out ferrous metals. These then pass onto a picking shed where they are further sorted by hand. Skilled operators pick out non-ferrous items and armatures that may inadvertently have been picked up by the overband magnet.

In the washing phase, light and absorbent materials are separated by the high-pressure jet of water. The dense media drum is filled with special liquids of varying density, which causes the materials to float off at different levels. In the second drum, medium density materials such as aluminium, stone and wire are separated from the heavier non-ferrous metals.

The aluminium is removed from the other medium density materials, such as stone and wire, using eddy currents. These are created by rapidly rotating magnets, which induce the aluminium fragments to leap away from the conveyor, while the stone and wire continue downwards. These techniques are mainly used for processing mixed metal waste from ELVs.

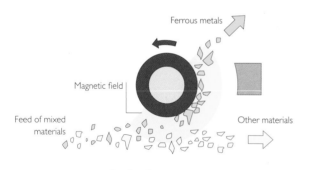

Overband magnet separator

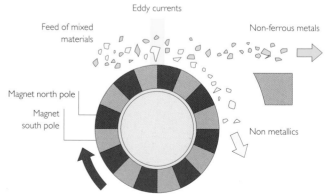

Washing

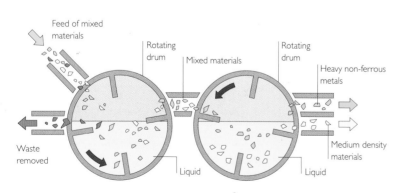

Dense media drum

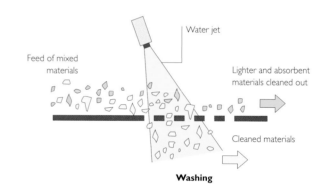

Eddy current separator

1

2

3

4

Separating Mixed Waste into Raw Materials

Featured company Sims Metal Management
www.simsmm.com

The shredded materials are loaded onto a conveyor (images **1** and **2**). Once the harmful and valuable materials have been removed by hand picking, the parts are broken into even smaller fragments (image **3**). This makes it possible to carry out the mechanical separation processes.

The materials pass through the series of processes such as the overband magnet, which removes material with iron content (image **4**). Once the materials have been processed and separated they are collected in piles (image **5**). This includes metals separated into the different types such as precious metals, copper alloys, aluminium alloys and steel.

Plastic materials are more difficult to split up and so are all collected together at this stage (image **6**). They have to be further separated if they are to be compounded back into raw materials that can be molded to make new products (Plastics Recycling, page 208).

5

6

Plastics Recycling

Plastics from mixed waste streams, such as packaging and construction, are recycled, extruded into raw material and molded into new products. Compared to virgin material, using recycled plastic reduces emissions (such as sulphur dioxide, carbon dioxide and nitrous oxide) and the consumption of energy, water and oil.

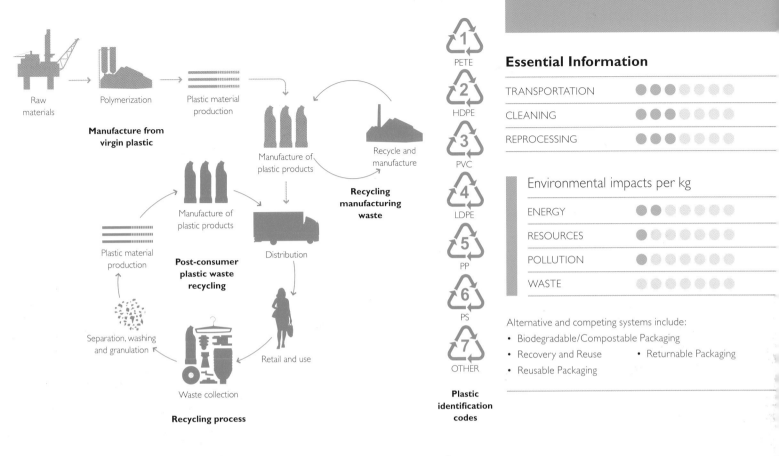

Raw materials

Polymerization

Plastic material production

Manufacture from virgin plastic

Manufacture of plastic products

Recycle and manufacture

Recycling manufacturing waste

Manufacture of plastic products

Plastic material production

Post-consumer plastic waste recycling

Distribution

Separation, washing and granulation

Retail and use

Waste collection

Recycling process

Plastic identification codes

1 PETE
2 HDPE
3 PVC
4 LDPE
5 PP
6 PS
7 OTHER

Essential Information

TRANSPORTATION	●●●●●○○
CLEANING	●●●●●○○
REPROCESSING	●●●●●○○

Environmental impacts per kg

ENERGY	●●●●●●●
RESOURCES	●●●●●●●
POLLUTION	●●●●●●●
WASTE	●●●●●●●

Alternative and competing systems include:
- Biodegradable/Compostable Packaging
- Recovery and Reuse
- Reusable Packaging
- Returnable Packaging

What is Plastics Recycling?

Mixed plastic waste is sorted and separated before it is recycled. This is important because different types of plastic do not mix well. In 1988 codes were established and they are still used to distinguish the seven different types: polyethylene terephthalate (PETE or PET), high density polyethylene (HDPE), polyvinyl chloride (PVC), low density polyethylene (LDPE), polypropylene (PP), polystyrene (PS) and others. Modern recycling facilities use sophisticated systems for identifying plastic types, such as light transmission, infrared, floatation and blowing.

Even with the latest automated sorting technologies it is still necessary to do a certain amount of hand sorting.

The separated plastic is cleaned and converted into flakes. It is melted, extruded and cut into pellets ready for molding into new products (see also, Molding Recycled Plastic, page 120). Scrap plastic is inevitable in most molding processes (such as start-up and offcuts), so many factories carry out on-site recycling to maximize efficiency. This type of material may be referred to as 'reprocessed' or 'regrind' rather than 'recycled'.

Notes for Designers

DESIGN Contamination from additives, such as fillers and dyes, will affect the quality. Improved separation systems have evolved to accommodate the wide range of mixed plastic materials. The efficiency and likelihood of plastic being recycled is increased by using a single type of material or enabling easy dismantling of parts into individual materials. This approach also aids recovery and reuse (page 186).

APPLICATIONS Plastics that are recycled can be used to make the same product again, such as detergent bottles, or returnable transit packaging (RTP) (see below), or they can be down-cycled into another type of product: for instance, HDPE can be turned into wood plastic composite (WPC) or PETE into polyester fleece. When the recycled material is used to make a new product that is of higher quality than the product from which it was derived it is known as upcycling. The most commonly recycled plastics are used in a range of applications: PETE for bottles and trays, HDPE for pipes, drums and bags, PVC for construction (flooring and window frames) and footwear, LDPE for bags and sheets, high impact polystyrene sheets (HIPS) for packaging and stationery, PP for automotive applications and horticultural products and PS for insulation and packaging.

COST The cost of recycled plastics is usually lower than virgin material. The process requires only 20% of the energy used to manufacture virgin plastic; using recycled plastics saves 1–3 tons of carbon dioxide equivalent emissions for every ton of virgin plastic that is replaced. Plastics must be very pure and free from metallic contamination or organic contaminants. Some recycled plastic has over 99.5% purity. Other products, such as mixed polypropylene (PP) and polyethylene (PE), may not be so pure because lower grades are less expensive and the quality is adequate for some applications. Also, less pure recycled plastic generates less waste during recycling.

Closed-loop Returnable transit packaging (RTP) is used to ship products, washed and reused. At the end of its useful life it is recycled into new RTP. This closed-loop approach to packaging significantly reduces waste and cost. It is estimated that a typical crate, such as those used by supermarkets to ship groceries, will be reused an average of 92 times before it needs to be recycled.

Colour Feedstock materials are sorted by colour as well as material type. Colour coding ranges from natural (no pigment added, such as milk container waste) to 'light jazz' (pastel mixed shades) and 'dark jazz' (stronger mixed colours) or they are separated into individual colour groups such as red, blue and black. This ensures that a wide colour range can be achieved. So, even if the colour range is not as wide as the one that can be achieved with virgin plastics, it is becoming less of an issue. Dark and strong colours will be the most successful.

Case Study

Recycling Mixed Plastic Waste

Featured company REGAIN Polymers Limited
www.regainpolymers.com

REGAIN Polymers specialize in recycling rigid plastic materials from post-consumer and industrial waste streams (image **1**). One ton (2,204 lbs) of plastic is equivalent to around 120,000 carrier bags or 20,000 two-litre (0.5 gallons) drink bottles. Producing one ton of carrier bags from recycled HDPE saves around 1.8 tons (3,968 lbs) of oil. In addition, this reduces the consumption of energy, water and emissions.

First the materials are sorted by type and colour – unless the material is from a consistent source. The plastic is washed if necessary and chopped into flakes (image **2**) approximately 1 cm² (0.15 in²). At this stage, different grades of plastic are combined according to the specific customer requirements. Colour, along with any other required additives, such as UV stabilizers and impact modifiers, is added during the extrusion process (image **3**). At the end of the extrusion line the plastic is cut into granules suitable for molding (image **4**).

1

2

3

4

Paper Recycling

Paper-based materials account for around one-third of the waste produced in the EU and US, by weight, which is more than any other material. Recycling reduces water and air pollution, reduces materials going to landfill, requires less energy than virgin pulp production and reduces the consumption of raw materials.

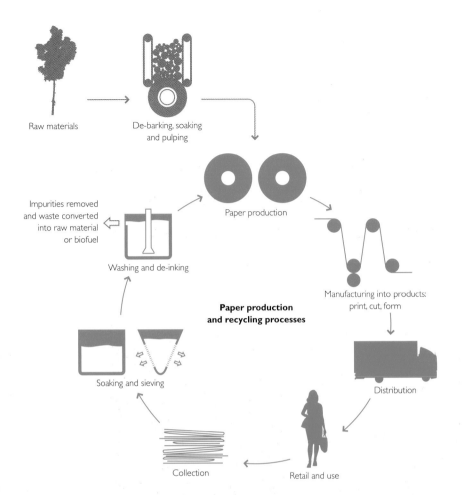

Raw materials

De-barking, soaking and pulping

Paper production

Impurities removed and waste converted into raw material or biofuel

Washing and de-inking

Paper production and recycling processes

Manufacturing into products: print, cut, form

Soaking and sieving

Distribution

Collection

Retail and use

Essential Information

TRANSPORTATION	●●●●○○○
CLEANING	●●●●●○○
REPROCESSING	●●○○○○○

Environmental impacts per kg

ENERGY	●●●○○○○
RESOURCES	●●○○○○○
POLLUTION	●●●○○○○
WASTE	●●○○○○○

Alternative and competing processes include:
- Biodegradable/Compostable Packaging
- Recovery and Reuse   • Returnable Packaging
- Reusable Packaging

What is Paper Recycling?

Paper is collected from households, offices and factories. In the US and Europe around two-thirds of paper is recycled and this continues to improve. It is graded according to quality and bound into large bales (see opposite). At the paper mill it is soaked and converted into pulp. It is screened (filtered), cleaned, de-inked and further screened until it is suitable for papermaking (page 74).

During recycling, the length of the wood fibres is slightly reduced each time. Therefore, many paper-based products are manufactured using a mix of recycled pulp with virgin material. Even so, many products, such as tissue, newspapers, magazines and corrugated containers, can be made from 100% recovered paper.

Even though paper-based products are biodegradable, it is typically more effective to recycle them because this saves resources, reduces energy consumption and diverts materials from landfill.

DESIGN The look, feel and performance (including colour) can be virtually indistinguishable from virgin pulp. However, heavily contaminated waste requires substantial reprocessing (including bleaching) to make bright white paper. The use of recovered paper is not always the preferred option if, for example, superior lightness and stiffness are required (see Pulp, Paper and Board, page 70).

APPLICATIONS There are several categories of pulp-based recovered materials such as corrugated, mixed, magazines, office waste, newspaper, high grade and pulp substitutes (such as waste from a sawmill, see Wood, page 56). Mixed materials are much

more difficult – and in some cases impossible – to recycle. For example, paper-based drink cartons are laminated with around 20% plastic and 5% aluminium (long-life products), making them impossible to recycle by conventional means.

Most paper products can be manufactured from recovered paper.

COST Recovered paper is a fundamental part of most modern papermaking and so the cost difference is not usually an issue. However, the total cost of recycling depends on availability, the efficiency of the mill and the level of contamination (including ink) on the recovered paper.

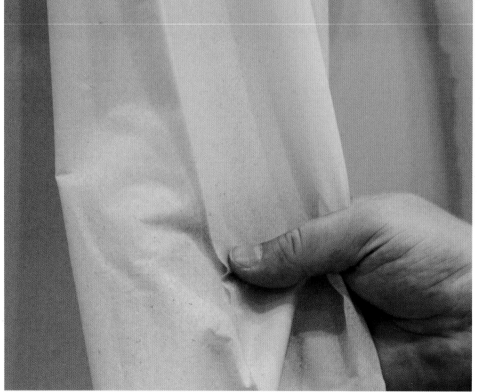

Metsä tissue Over 50% of the raw material in this tissue is from recovered paper. Chemicals are used to improve the efficiency of its manufacturing processes. An example is the soap used during the de-inking process. Chemicals are also added to achieve certain desired qualities such as wet strength adhesive (for paper towels) or silicone (non-stick surfaces on baking paper) in the end product. All the chemicals used in their products and production processes are safe for people and the environment. They fulfil the environmental criteria of the Nordic Ecolabel, EU Ecolabel, Germany's BfR (Federal Institute for Risk Assessment) and USA's FDA (US Food and Drug Administration).

1

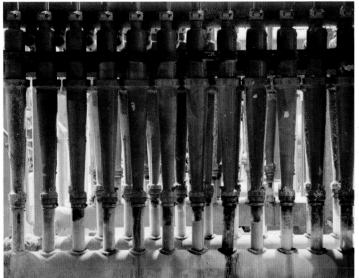

2

3

4

5

Case Study

Paper Recycling in Tissue Production

Featured company Metsä Tissue
www.metsatissue.com

Recovered pulp passes through the same process as virgin pulp (page 70). The difference is that recycled pulp has to be sorted and cleaned prior to conversion into paper. It is soaked and pulped (image **1**). Contamination, such as staples and string, is removed by screening (filtering) and centrifugal force (image **2**).

The pulp is mixed with hot water and chemicals (see opposite). Using froth flotation, printing ink is removed from the fibres by rising air bubbles blown in from underneath. Waste from the de-inking process, called sludge, is used as a raw material (such as aggregate for road building) or converted into biofuel and burnt to produce energy (image **3**).

The pulp is diluted with water, mixed with 50% virgin pulp (the amount depends on the application and can be up to 100%), and passed through a series of screens to make it suitable for papermaking (images **4** and **5**).

Glass Recycling

Glass can be recycled in a virtual closed-loop system, over and over again without any loss of quality. Due to the inherent value of glass, recycling schemes are widespread and as a result blown-glass packaging typically contains around one-third recycled material.

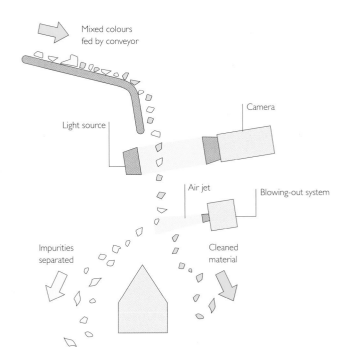

Mixed colours
fed by conveyor

Camera

Light source

Air jet

Blowing-out system

Impurities
separated

Cleaned
material

Essential Information

TRANSPORTATION	●●●○○○○
CLEANING	●●●●○○○
REPROCESSING	●●○○○○○

Environmental impacts per kg

ENERGY	●●○○○○○
RESOURCES	●○○○○○○
POLLUTION	●○○○○○○
WASTE	●○○○○○○

Alternative and competing systems include:
- Returnable Packaging

What is Colour Separation in Glass Recycling?

Many of the processes used in glass recycling are the same as for mixed recycling (page 198). The mixed waste is crushed and cleaned through vibrating screens. Magnets, flotation and eddy currents are employed to separate the metals (ferrous and non-ferrous), paper and other impurities. In addition, sophisticated x-ray inspection identifies potentially troublesome and otherwise undetectable contaminants such as ceramic and borosilicate glass ovenware, which are removed.

The clear, green and amber glass is sorted in the colour separation unit. The crushed glass is fed into the process by a vibrating conveyor to ensure it is evenly distributed. It falls through an illumination section where it is backlit with white light and a camera identifies the RGB spectra. The particles are separated by an air jet pulse, which forces them to fall into designated chutes. Recycling 1 ton (2,204 lbs) of glass saves more than 300 kg (661 lbs) carbon dioxide equivalent emissions.

Notes for Designers

DESIGN   Glass is a versatile material that can be molded, etched, coloured and decorated. As long as the parts can be separated (such as caps and labels) the glass can be recycled. The colour affects the amount of recycled content that can be used. For the manufacture of green glass bottles, up to 90% cullet can be used. For clear glass, small amounts of colour contamination are chemically removed during glassblowing (see below, left).

APPLICATIONS   Glass bottles and jars are used to package many products including food, drink, medicines and cosmetics. Soda-lime glass is also used to make windows in buildings (page 55) and light bulbs, for example. Low quality recycled glass is employed to make aggregate and composite glass panels (such as countertops). Blue Carpet, designed by Heatherwick Studio for Newcastle City Council, UK, is made of crushed blue Harvey's Bristol Cream sherry bottles in white resin.

COST   Cullet is fundamental in the manufacture of commodity glass products such as jars and bottles. Separating and recycling glass significantly reduces materials going to landfill since glass is often more substantial than plastic equivalents.

Mass production glassblowing The furnace-ready cullet is combined with silica sand, dolomite, lime and soda. The raw materials are melted, mixed and formed by glassblowing – using a combination of air pressure and press molding – into jars and bottles.

Glass defects It only takes a small amount of contamination to cause defects in blown glass. Materials including ceramic and borosilicate glass (such as that used in cookware) are particularly tricky because they are difficult to identify and separate during recycling.

1

2

3

4

5

Case Study

Converting Mixed Glass Waste into Cullet

Featured company Berryman Glass Recycling
www.berrymanglassrecycling.com

Waste glass comes from bottle banks, roadside collection or factory scrap. It is a mixture of different colours, chemical compositions, bottles with metal or plastic caps and other contaminants (image **1**).

The materials are crushed and the metals (image **2**) and plastics are removed for separate recycling (page 208). The glass goes through machines that use laser, x-ray and digital technology (images **3** and **4**) to remove contaminants such as ceramic, stone and glass with different chemical compositions. It can also distinguish between colours and types of glass. As it falls, each fragment is scanned and identified and the information fed into a computer, which activates air jets lower down. These jets are fired at the specified piece of contamination or glass with pinpoint accuracy, blasting them onto separate conveyor belts. In this way, the green, brown and clear glass can be separated out.

The recycled material, known as furnace-ready cullet (image **5**), is soda-lime glass. Other types of glass have to be removed and recycled separately because they behave differently when molded (in terms of their melting point and coefficient of expansion, see opposite).

Index